Key Skills

Communication

Jane Williams

Hodder & Stoughton

A MEMBER OF THE HODDER HEADLINE GROUP

Every effort has been made to trace copyright holders of material reproduced in this book. Any rights omitted from the acknowledgements here or in the text will be added for subsequent printings following notice to the publisher.

Photographs appear courtesy of:
Mary Evans picture library 100; PA Photos 65 158 160 161; Hulton Getty 117; Guzelien 202; The Daily Mirror 200; Chris Neill 122; Express Newspapers 197.

Cover Illustration by Stewart Larkin
Illustrations by Karen Donnelly

Orders: please contact Bookpoint Ltd, 130 Milton Park, Abingdon, Oxon OX14 4SB. Telephone (44) 01235 827720, Fax: (44) 01235 400454. Lines are open from 9.00–6.00, Monday to Saturday, with a 24 hour message answering service. E-mail address: orders@bookpoint.co.uk

British Library cataloguing in Publication Data
A catalogue record for this title is available from The British Library

ISBN 0 340 801492

Typeset by Wyvern 21 Ltd, Bristol
Printed in Great Britain for Hodder & Stoughton Educational, a division of Hodder Headline PLC, 338 Euston Road, London NW1 3BH by Bath Press Ltd.

Contents

Welcome to Key Skills Communication

This book is one of three in the *Key Skills Builder* series, and is designed to help you understand, develop and apply your Communication skills to nationally recognised standards. Step by step, this book will help you improve your understanding of what you need to know and do, in order to successfully achieve a Key Skills Unit Qualification in Communication at either Level 1, 2 or 3.

Who needs Key Skills?

It might surprise you to learn that *everybody* needs key skills. This is because they form an important part of work, study and everyday life, for everyone. Although there are a total of six key skills, the *Key Skills Builder* series concentrates on three. These are:

- Communication
- Application of Number
- Information Technology

Each of these key skills is assessed through the production of a portfolio and by taking a test. As a result, each of them can be regarded as a qualification in its own right. Together they also make up a completely new, nationally recognised qualification called the Key Skills Qualification.

It is important to remember that there are also three other key skills. These are:

- Working with Others
- Improving Own Learning and Performance
- Problem Solving

These are often referred to as personal skills and, unlike the other three, are assessed only through the production of a portfolio.

Getting the measure of Key Skills

The ability to communicate, use numbers and use computers is so much a part of everyday life, that most people take these skills completely for granted. Perhaps it is for this reason that we rarely stop to consider these skills, or how important they are in all our lives.

For some time, the government and employers have been concerned that many people cannot use academic skills in practical situations. For example, someone who has a good grade in GCSE maths may find it difficult to work out the profit margin on a particular product, or someone who has passed 'A' Level English finds it difficult to write formal reports for their manager at work.

In order to address these concerns, the regulatory authorities in England, Wales and Northern Ireland (QCA, ACCAC & CCEA) have published specifications for each of the key skills units, describing in detail what candidates need to know, and do, at each level. These units set national standards, which candidates can measure their performance against.

In order to show your abilities in Communication you will need to learn more about what is involved (*check your skills*), develop the skills needed to be able to use your knowledge effectively (*practise your skills*), then undertake activities that will allow you to demonstrate your competence (*apply your skills*).

It is important to remember that everybody is different, and that we all find some skills harder to apply than others. With this in mind the key skills units have been written at different levels, in order to accommodate those with a basic grasp of the skill to those who can apply the skill in much more complex ways.

Whilst there are also key skills units at Levels 4 and 5, these are aimed at graduate level candidates, and are not covered in this particular book.

Achieving a Key Skills Qualification

Whether your target is one, two, or all three units it is important that you work towards the most suitable level for your own needs. This might well mean that you work towards different key skills at different levels (ie Number and Communication at Level 2 and IT at Level 3), therefore it is important that you start by discussing your plans with your tutor. Having established the most appropriate level for each key skill you will also need to decide/agree the most suitable contexts in which you could develop and demonstrate the skills.

For those at school or college these might include academic or vocational subjects (GCSEs, A/AS Levels, GNVQs, AVEs etc), entitlement or enrichment programmes (PSHE, citizenship, careers etc), community activities (voluntary work, youth work, charitable work etc). Those in training or employment might well identify suitable contexts from within their working environment, whilst candidates from all backgrounds could identify suitable extra curricular and leisure activities (Duke of Edinburgh's Award, Young Enterprise, sport, music, drama productions etc, community activities, voluntary work, youth work, charitable work etc). Opportunities to develop and apply key skills exist almost everywhere.

Using this book

This book contains information that will help you to decide just how much you already know and how much you still need to learn about Communication at each level. It describes activities that other students have used to help them develop their own skills, and includes examples of the types of evidence they produced for their portfolios. It includes checklists and action plans, and provides guidance on how to put together your portfolio and how to prepare for the tests.

Key Skills Communication is designed to be used flexibly, so you can either follow the whole process through at a particular level, or dip in and out of appropriate sections as the need arises. Whether used as a structured programme of skills development, or simply as a source of information, ideas and guidance, make sure that you discuss with your tutor or supervisor how to make best use of Key Skills Communication.

Introduction to Communication

Why do we need Communication Skills?

Communication skills are essential in every part of our daily lives. Whether speaking to friends to arrange an evening out, reading a magazine, or writing an assignment for school or college, good communication skills are needed. This book is designed to give you support and guidance as you develop, practise and demonstrate your communication skills.

But what are Communication skills?

By communication skills we mean speaking, listening, reading and writing skills.

How can this book help me develop my Communication skills?

This book will help you to check that you have the knowledge and skills needed in Communication. It will also help you to demonstrate that you can apply these skills in different situations. You will first need to decide which level is best for you based on your current experience. This book will help you to do this. This will give you the best opportunity to achieve in Communication, either as a single unit or as part of The Key Skills Qualification.

How will I be assessed in Communication?

As a communication candidate you will be assessed in two ways before you can be given a QCA certificate:

1. **You will complete a test (this is the external assessment).**

2. **You will build a portfolio of evidence (this is the internal assessment).**

▶ DEFINITIONS ▶

CANDIDATE: Anyone registered for one or more Key Skills units. You must be registered before you can receive a certificate.

QCA: The Qualifications and Curriculum Authority, the Government organisation which has written the Key Skills units, and has decided on how they should be assessed.

ASSESSMENT: The ways in which the skills and knowledge you have are tested and marked.

PORTFOLIO: File of evidence which proves the things you say you can do are true.

EVIDENCE: This could be written work, posters, computer printouts, video, tape, all of which show your skills and knowledge.

LEVEL: The Key Skill unit Communication can be achieved at levels 1-4.

EXTERNAL ASSESSMENT: Test which is either multiple choice, at levels 1 and 2, or written at level 3.

INTERNAL ASSESSMENT: The portfolio of evidence.

The Communication Unit

Like all the Key Skills units, Communication can be achieved at levels 1–4. At each level the Communication unit has four parts:

1. **An overview**

2. **Part A – what you need to know**

3. **Part B – what you must do**

4. **Part C – guidance**

These four parts are explained overleaf:

1. An overview

This is a very short summary of the unit.

2. Part A – what you need to know

This is the knowledge you must have, and the skills you must practise.

You will need to be able to do all the points shown. There are examples of how you could achieve them. You do not have to show evidence of covering every example. A range of examples are given to guide you, and to give you ideas of your own.

You will be assessed on Part A in your written test. This is set by an Awarding Body, and taken under supervised conditions.

3. Part B – what you must do

This is the evidence you must produce to show that you have the Communication skills and knowledge at your chosen level. This evidence shows that you can apply your skills and knowledge to everyday situations. Part B tells you how much evidence you need, and the type of evidence required. It also gives the criteria you must meet in your portfolio evidence.

This portfolio of evidence will be assessed and checked before you can receive a Communication certificate.

Part C – Guidance

This gives you some ideas about the types of activities and evidence you could use. This evidence will show that you have the knowledge and skills set out in the unit, at the level you are working.

DEFINITIONS ▶

CRITERIA: the standards you must reach in the test, and in your portfolio. If you do not do well enough to meet the criteria you will not get a certificate.

AWARDING BODY: The exam board with whom you are registered, which sets and marks the tests, and checks the portfolio e.g. AQA, ASDAN, Edexcel, OCR.

Communication unit at levels 1, 2 and 3

You can move up through the Key Skills levels in the following ways:

- Carry out more complex tasks, in a wider variety of situations.
- Take more responsibility for planning, and decision making when carrying out tasks and solving problems.
- Evaluate your own performance, and understand the reasons for difficulties and successes when solving problems.

If you are working at level 2, you will need to be able to do all the things set out in level 1, and the additional parts of level 2, shown in italics.

If you are working at level 3, you will be able to do all the things set out in level 2, and the additional parts of level 3, shown in italics.

Level 1

This level is roughly equivalent to other national qualifications, such as NVQ 1, Foundation GNVQ or GCSE grades D–G. You may be able to achieve Communication at a higher level, even though your main programme of study is at level 1.

Speaking and Listening

At level 1 you should be able to develop the ability to speak with confidence about everyday subjects. You must be able to speak clearly, using gestures and tone to emphasise your points. You should also be able to show you are listening, by using body language, or by asking questions and making sensible comments.

Reading

You must be able to read specific books, articles or reports given to you, and to pick out the main points in straightforward material, including points made using images. You must then be able to put the information you have together, and use it.

Writing

You should be able to write about everyday topics, using images to show the main points. Your sentences must be spelt and punctuated correctly.

Level 2

This level is roughly equivalent to other national qualifications, such as NVQ 2, Intermediate GNVQ or GCSE grades A*–C. You may be trying to achieve Communication at a higher or lower level, even though your main programme of study is at level 2.

Speaking and Listening

At level 2 you must be able to take part in discussions about everyday subjects, but also to *take responsibility for moving the discussion forward, by summarising and questioning. You must also be able to prepare for, and give, a short talk using an image to explain your main points. The talk should last 5–6 minutes, and the audience should be at least two or three people whom you know.*

Reading

You must be able to read and *summarise information, from extended documents, which are at least three pages long. You should understand the writer's opinions and point of view.*

Writing

You must choose and use different styles of writing to suit specific purposes, making decisions about how to best structure your work. You must be able to write *extended documents* about everyday subjects, using images to show the main points. You must be able to spell and punctuate correctly *when writing complex sentences.*

Level 3

This level is roughly equivalent to other national qualifications, such as NVQ 3, Advanced GNVQ or GCE AS/A level. You may be trying to achieve Communication at a different level, even though your main programme of study is at level 3.

Speaking and Listening

At level 3 you must be able to contribute to discussions yourself, and *create openings for others to contribute. The topics of discussion should be complex, technical or concerning sensitive issues.* You must also be able to prepare for, and give, *a presentation which is well structured, and engages the audience.*

Reading

You must be able to read, summarise and *synthesise information*, from extended documents, *which you have identified yourself as useful to your subject. You must give your own interpretation of a complex subject, taking account of the opinions of the writers.*

Writing

You must choose and use different styles of writing to suit specific purposes, making decisions about how best to structure your work. You must be able to write extended documents *about complex topics* using images to show the main points. You must be able to spell and punctuate correctly *when writing complex sentences.*

In order to achieve the Communication unit you will need to:

- Be registered as a Key Skills candidate.
- Complete an initial assessment, to check the skills and knowledge that you have, and to find out where there are gaps.
- Decide which level is best for you, with the help of your tutor/teacher/supervisor/assessor.
- Begin a structured programme, which is designed to help you develop and practise your communication skills, using real examples and situations which are helpful to you.
- Make sure that you have all the skills and knowledge set out in Part A of the unit.
- Practise and prepare for the test, which will be based on Part A.
- Pass the test.
- Carry out activities and tasks which show you can apply your skills in new situations.
- Collect a portfolio of evidence, which is well organised and which covers all of Part B of the unit.
- Have your portfolio assessed and checked as having enough evidence at the right standard.
- Receive your certificate in Communication.

■ NOTE: You will be working on both Part A and Part B at the same time in your course or programme. You do not have to pass the test, before your portfolio is assessed. You will, however, need to have developed and practised your skills before you take the test or put your portfolio together.

Summary of the Communication unit

- Communication skills are: Speaking, Listening, Reading, Writing
- The Communication unit has been written at levels 1–4
- This book will help you at levels 1–3
- At each level of Communication there are four parts:
→ An overview
→ Part A which explains what you need to know
→ Part B which sets out what you must do
→ Part C which gives you some guidance on how to achieve the unit

You will be assessed in two ways:

1. By sitting a test

2. By building a portfolio of evidence

DEFINITIONS ▶

IMAGES: Pictures, charts, diagrams, sketches.

EXTENDED DOCUMENTS: At least three pages long.

Introduction to Levels 1-3

Level 1

At this level you must be able to:

- Take part in discussions about straightforward subjects.
- Read and identify the main points and ideas from documents about straightforward subjects.
- Write about straightforward subjects.

This means that you must be able to use speaking, listening, reading and writing skills in ordinary tasks. You must be able to take part in everyday discussions, pick out the main points when you are reading familiar materials, and write short documents using simple words.

Key Skills: Communication Unit: Level 1 specification

Part A

WHAT YOU NEED TO KNOW

In discussions,

YOU NEED TO KNOW HOW TO:

- find out about the subject so you can say things that are relevant;
- judge when to speak and how much to say;
- say things that suit the purpose of the discussion (e.g. describe events, express opinions, develop ideas);
- speak clearly in a way that suits the situation (e.g. use appropriate tone of voice, expressions and manner to suit the formality of the situation, use language that everyone can understand);
- show you are listening closely to what others say (e.g. use body language, ask questions, make relevant comments, follow instructions, take messages).

In reading and obtaining information,

YOU NEED TO KNOW HOW TO:

- obtain advice from others on what to read for different purposes (e.g. to get instructions, facts, opinions, ideas);
- identify the main points and ideas in different types of straightforward material (e.g. letters, memos, extracts from books, newspaper or magazine articles), including images (e.g. pictures, charts, diagrams, sketches);

- use a dictionary;
- ask others when you are unclear about what you have read;
- prepare information so it is suitable for use (e.g. collate information as notes to use in discussions or written material such as a letter or short essay).

In writing documents,

YOU NEED TO KNOW HOW TO:

- use different written forms of presenting information (e.g. business letters, memos, application forms, notes, short reports or essays);
- use images to help the reader understand your main points (e.g. pictures, charts, diagrams, sketches);
- judge the relevance of information and the amount to include for your purpose (e.g. to give or obtain facts, opinions, ideas);
- make your meaning clear by writing, proofreading and re-drafting documents so that:
→ words you use most often in your work or studies are spelled correctly;
→ sentences are formed correctly (e.g. with subject-verb agreement such as 'she was', 'we were', with consistent use of tense);
→ sentences are marked by capital letters, full stops and question marks and organised into paragraphs where appropriate.

Part B

WHAT YOU MUST DO

You must:	*Evidence must show you can:*
C1.1 Take part in a **one-to-one** discussion and a **group** discussion about different, straightforward subjects.	• **provide information that is relevant to the subject and purpose of the discussion;** • **speak clearly in a way that suits the situation; and** • **listen and respond appropriately to what others say.**
C1.2 Read and obtain information from **two** different types of documents about straightforward subjects, including at least **one** image.	• **read relevant material;** • **identify accurately the main points and ideas in material; and** • **use the information to suit your purpose.**
C1.3 Write **two** different types of documents about straightforward subjects. Include at least **one** image in one of the documents.	• **present relevant information in a form that suits your purpose;** • **ensure text is legible; and** • **make sure that spelling, punctuation and grammar are accurate so your meaning is clear.**

To help you check whether level 1 is best for you, try to answer the questions below, as honestly as you can, and tick the boxes. Ask your teacher/supervisor for help if you need it.

Initial Self-assessment for Communication Level 1

Discussions (speaking and listening)

Can you:

Find out about the topic for discussion, by looking in books, magazines, newspapers, and other useful sources?
◯ YES   ◯ NO

Pick out the main points you want to make during the discussion?
◯ YES   ◯ NO

Make your points clearly, so that other people can understand you?
◯ YES   ◯ NO

Show you are listening to other people by asking sensible questions, and by your body language?
◯ YES   ◯ NO

Give an example of a discussion you have taken part in, within the last six months:
Topic:

Who took part:

The reason for the discussion:

Reading

Can you:

Follow instructions and ask for advice, when you are using books, magazines, newspapers, or other useful sources, to find out information?
◯ YES   ◯ NO

Pick out the main points from letters, memos, books, graphs, pictures or newspapers?
◯ YES   ◯ NO

Use a dictionary?
◯ YES   ◯ NO

Make notes, so that you can use them in a discussion, or to write a letter, or report?
◯ YES   ◯ NO

Give an example of reading and finding information that you have carried out in the last six months:

Topic:

The reason for your search:

The type of record you kept of your findings e.g. notes, report, summary:

Writing

Can you:

Write the following types of document:

Formal letters e.g. asking for information about a job? ◯ YES   ◯ NO

Memos? ◯ YES   ◯ NO

Application forms e.g. for a driving licence? ◯ YES   ◯ NO

Notes? ◯ YES   ◯ NO

Reports? ◯ YES   ◯ NO

Essays? ◯ YES   ◯ NO

Use pictures, charts and diagrams to make points in your written work?

◯ YES   ◯ NO

Make your written work easy to understand by:

Spelling everyday words correctly? ◯ YES   ◯ NO

Writing simple sentences correctly? ◯ YES   ◯ NO

Using capital letters, full stops and question marks correctly?

◯ YES   ◯ NO

Using headings and paragraphs? ◯ YES   ◯ NO

Give examples of two documents, which you have written in the last six months:

Topic: 1.

                          2.

Type of document: 1.

                          2.

Reason for writing it: 1.

                          2.

What the Self-assessment shows you:

If you have answered 'YES' to most or all of the questions, and have been able to give examples in each case, you should be able to achieve Communication at level 1. You may think that level 1 would be too easy, and that you ought to be working at the next level, level 2.

Check this with your teacher/supervisor.
If you have answered 'YES' to some of the questions, but there are some things you cannot do yet, you might think that this is definitely the right level for you to work at.
Check this with your teacher/supervisor.
If you have answered 'NO' to most or all of the questions, you may not be ready to try this level of Communication yet.

In order to achieve Communication at level 1 you will need to:

- Make sure that you can do all the points in Part A.
- Practise and prepare for the test.
- Pass the test at level 1 (external assessment, set and marked by the Awarding Body).
- Collect a portfolio of evidence, which is well organised, and which shows you can do all of Part B of the unit.
- Have your portfolio assessed and checked as having enough evidence at the right standard (internal assessment, carried out by your teacher/supervisor, and checked by the Awarding Body).

Summary of Communication level 1

This Key Skills unit is equivalent to NVQ 1, Foundation GNVQ, or GCSE grades D–G:

Speaking, listening, reading and writing skills are needed for everyday, routine activities.

Assessment:
External test: set and marked by Awarding Body
→ Test is one hour long
→ Questions are multiple choice
→ Up to 40 questions
→ Based on Part A

■ NOTE: You may be exempt from the test if you have already achieved GCSE grades D–G within the last three years.

Check this with your teacher/supervisor.

Internal portfolio: assessed within your school/college/ centre:
- Must cover all of Part B
- Must meet the standard
- Must be well organised

Level 2

At this level you must be able to:

- Help move discussions forward.
- Give a short talk using an image to illustrate your main points.
- Read and summarise information from extended documents (at least three pages long).
- Use a suitable structure and style when writing extended documents.

This means you must be able to use speaking, listening reading and writing skills in everyday situations. You must be able to take part in discussions, give a short talk, summarise the main points from longer documents, and write extended documents.

Key Skills: Communication Unit: Level 2 specification

Part A

WHAT YOU NEED TO KNOW

In discussions,
YOU NEED TO KNOW HOW TO:

- use varied vocabulary and expressions to suit your purpose *(e.g. to present an argument, express ideas or opinions, exchange information)*;
- adapt your contributions to suit different situations *(e.g. the amount you say, your manner and tone of voice)*;
- show you are listening closely *(e.g. by body language)* and respond appropriately *(e.g. make tactful comments, ask questions to show interest)*;
- identify the speaker's intentions *(e.g. by manner, tone of voice, vocabulary)*;
- move the discussion forward *(e.g. summarise, develop points, focus on purpose)*.

In giving a short talk,
YOU NEED TO KNOW HOW TO:

- prepare for the talk *(e.g. research the topic, make notes, choose images)*;
- adapt your language to suit your subject, purpose and situation *(e.g. use standard English, avoid or explain technical terms, keep attention by varying tone of voice, giving examples)*;
- structure what you say to help listeners follow a line of thought or series of events *(e.g. by signalling new points: firstly ... , secondly ... and finally)*;
- use images to help others understand the main points of your talk *(e.g. a model, picture, sketch plan or diagram to show what you mean)*.

In reading and summarising information,
YOU NEED TO KNOW HOW TO:

- use different sources to obtain relevant information *(e.g. to obtain and compare facts, opinions or ideas, obtain instructions or directions)*;

- skim materials to gain a general idea of content and scan text to identify the information you need from straightforward, extended documents *(e.g. reports, text books, articles of more than three pages with key points easily identified)*;
- recognise the writer's intentions *(e.g. by tone, vocabulary, structure of text)*;
- identify main lines of reasoning *(e.g. by signal words such as 'therefore', 'so', 'whereas')* and main points from text and images *(e.g. pictures, charts, diagrams)*;
- summarise information for a purpose *(e.g. a talk or written report)*.

In writing documents,
YOU NEED TO KNOW HOW TO:

- present written information in different forms *(e.g. letters, memos, extended documents such as essays or reports of more than three pages)*, including images *(e.g. pictures, sketches, charts, diagrams)*;
- structure your material to help readers follow what you have written and understand the main points *(e.g. use paragraphs, headings and sub-headings)*;
- use different styles of writing to suit different purposes *(e.g. persuasive techniques to present arguments, technical vocabulary, supporting evidence for reports)*;
- make meaning clear by writing, proof-reading and re-drafting documents so that:
→ words most often used in your work or studies are spelled correctly and spelling of irregular words is checked *(e.g. use a dictionary or spell-checker)*;
→ complex sentences are formed correctly *(e.g. use of 'but', 'then', 'because', consistent use of tense)* and organised into paragraphs where appropriate;
→ punctuation is accurate *(e.g. use of commas, apostrophes, inverted commas)*.

Part **B**

WHAT YOU MUST DO

You must:

Evidence must show you can:

C2.1a
Contribute to a discussion about a straightforward subject.

- make clear and relevant contributions in a way that suits your purpose and situation;
- listen and respond appropriately to what others say; and
- help to move the discussion forward.

C2.1b
Give a short talk about a straightforward subject, using an image.

- speak clearly in a way that suits your subject, purpose and situation;
- keep to the subject and structure your talk to help listeners follow what you are saying; and
- use an image to clearly illustrate your main points.

C2.2
Read and summarise information from **two** extended documents about a straightforward subject. One of the documents should include at least **one** image.

- select and read relevant material;
- identify accurately the lines of reasoning and main points from text and images; and
- summarise the information to suit your purpose.

C2.3
Write **two** different types of documents about straightforward subjects.
One piece of writing should be an extended document and include at least **one** image.

- present relevant information in an appropriate from;
- use a structure and style of writing to suit your purpose; and
- ensure text is legible and that spelling, punctuation and grammar are accurate, so your meaning is clear.

To help you check whether level 2 is the best one for you to work at, try to answer the questions below, as honestly as you can, and tick the boxes. Ask your teacher/supervisor for help if you need it.

Initial Self-assessment for Communication Level 2

Discussions (speaking and listening)

Can you:

Use a variety of words and expressions, adapting what you say to suit the situation?
◯ YES ◯ NO

Show you are listening closely, by asking questions and by your body language?
◯ YES ◯ NO

Move the discussion forward by summarising, and building on points made?
◯ YES ◯ NO

Give an example of a discussion you have taken part in, within the last six months:

Topic:

Who took part:

The reason for the discussion:

Giving a short talk (Speaking)

Can you:

Research the topic of the talk, and make notes of the main points?
◯ YES ◯ NO

Use suitable language to suit the topic and audience, e.g. without using slang, and by keeping people's attention?
◯ YES ◯ NO

Structure your talk, so that listeners can follow your points in a logical order?
◯ YES ◯ NO

Use images e.g. pictures, diagrams, plans or a model to help make the main points?
◯ YES ◯ NO

Give an example of a talk you have given in the last six months:

Topic:

Audience:

Reason for the talk:

Reading

Can you:

Use books, magazines, reports or other sources to find useful information?
◯ YES ◯ NO

Skim and scan extended documents, at least three pages long, to pick out the main points, and the writer's opinions and arguments?
◯ YES ◯ NO

Pick out the main points and the lines of reasoning, from text and images?
◯ YES ◯ NO

Summarise information to use for a talk, or to write a report?
◯ YES ◯ NO

Give an example of reading and summarising information that you have carried out in the last six months:

Topic:

The reason for your search:

The type of record you kept of your findings e.g. notes, report, summary.

Writing   .

Can you write the following types of document:

Letters? ◯ YES ◯ NO

Memos? ◯ YES ◯ NO

Essays of more than three pages? ◯ YES ◯ NO

Reports of more than three pages? ◯ YES ◯ NO

Notes? ◯ YES ◯ NO

Application forms? ◯ YES ◯ NO

Use images (pictures, charts, diagrams, sketches) to make points in your written work?
◯ YES ◯ NO

Use different styles of writing to suit your purpose e.g. presenting an argument, writing a technical report?
◯ YES ◯ NO

Use a dictionary or spell-checker?

◯ YES   ◯ NO

Make your written work easy to understand by:

Spelling everyday and unusual words correctly? ◯ YES   ◯ NO

Writing complicated sentences e.g. which include 'but' or 'because'?

◯ YES   ◯ NO

Using commas, apostrophes and inverted commas correctly?

◯ YES   ◯ NO

Using headings, paragraphs and sub-headings? ◯ YES   ◯ NO

Give examples of two extended documents, which you have written in the last six months:

Topic: 1.

                   2.

Type of document: 1.

                   2.

Reason for writing it: 1.

                        2.

What the Self-assessment shows you:

If you have answered 'YES' to most or all of the questions, and have been able to give examples in each case, you should be able to achieve Communication at level 2. You may think that level 2 would be too easy and that you ought to be working at the next level, level 3.

Check this with your teacher/supervisor.
If you have answered 'YES' to some of the questions, but there are some things you cannot do yet, you might think that this is definitely the right level for you to work at.

Check this with your teacher/supervisor.
If you have answered 'NO' to most or all of the questions, you may not be ready to try this level of Communication. You may need to start at level 1. Try the self-assessment at level 1 to find out.

In order to achieve Communication at level 2 you will need to:

- Make sure that you can do all the points in Part A.
- Practise and prepare for the test.
- Pass the test at level 2 (external assessment, set and marked by the Awarding Body).
- Collect a portfolio of evidence, which is well organised, and which shows you can do all of Part B of the unit.
- Have your portfolio assessed and checked as having enough evidence at the right standard (internal assessment, carried out by your teacher/supervisor, and checked by the Awarding Body).

Summary of Communication level 2

This Key Skills unit is equivalent to NVQ 2, Intermediate GNVQ, or GCSE grades A*–C

Speaking, listening, reading and writing skills are needed for everyday, routine activities, involving extended documents.

Assessment:
External test: set and marked by Awarding Body

- → Test is one hour long
- → Questions are multiple choice
- → Up to 40 questions
- → Based on Part A

■ NOTE: You may be exempt from the test if you have already achieved GCSE grades A*–C within the last three years.

Check this with your teacher/supervisor.

Internal portfolio: assessed within your school/college/centre:
- Must cover all of Part B
- Must meet the standard
- Must be well organised

Level 3

At this level you must be able to:

- Create opportunities for others to contribute to group discussions about complex subjects.
- Make a presentation using a range of techniques to engage the audience.
- Read and synthesise information from extended documents about a complex subject.
- Organise information coherently, selecting a form and style of writing appropriate to complex subject matter.

This means you must be able to use speaking, listening, reading and writing skills in more involved ways, and in unfamiliar situations. You must be able to take part in discussions, and to make a presentation, about a sensitive or complex issue. You must also be able to synthesise information from extended documents, of at least three pages, and to write complex, extended documents in a coherent way.

Key Skills: Communication Unit: Level 3 specifications

Part A

WHAT YOU NEED TO KNOW

In discussions:
YOU NEED TO KNOW HOW TO:

- vary how and when you participate to suit your purpose (e.g. to present a complicated line of reasoning or argument, explain events, express opinions and ideas) and the situation (e.g. formality, nature of the group);
- listen and respond sensitively (e.g. acknowledge gender and cultural aspects, how others might be feeling) and develop points and ideas;
- make openings to encourage others to contribute (e.g. invite others to speak, ask follow-up questions to encourage people to develop points).

In making a presentation,
YOU NEED TO KNOW HOW TO:

- prepare the presentation to suit your purpose (e.g. present an argument in a debate, findings from an investigation, outcomes from a design brief);
- match your language and style to suit the complexity of the subject, the formality of the situation and the needs of the audience (e.g. confidently use standard English, precisely use vocabulary);
- structure what you say (e.g. help listeners follow the sequence of mains points, ideas);
- use techniques to engage the audience, including images (e.g. give examples to illustrate complex points, relate what is said to audience experience, vary tone of voice, use images, such as charts, pictures and models to illustrate points).

In reading and synthesising information,
YOU NEED TO KNOW HOW TO:

- find and skim read extended documents, such as text books, secondary sources,

articles and reports, to identify relevant material (e.g. to extend thinking around a subject, obtain evidence, opinions and ideas);
- scan and read the material to find the specific information you need;
- use appropriate sources of reference to help you understand complex lines of reasoning and information from text and images (e.g. consult databases and other texts, ask others for clarification);
- compare accounts and recognise opinion and possible bias (e.g. identify the writer's intentions by the way meaning and information is conveyed);
- synthesise the information you have obtained for a purpose (e.g. present your own interpretation of the subject in a way that brings information together in a coherent form for a report or presentation).

In writing documents,
YOU NEED TO KNOW HOW TO:

- select appropriate forms for presenting information (e.g. extended essay or report, images, such as pictures, charts and diagrams) to suit your purpose (e.g. present an argument, ideas, a complicated line of reasoning or a series of events);
- select appropriate styles to suit the degree of formality required and nature of the subject (e.g. use vocabulary, sentence structures and tone that suit the intended readers and the complexity or sensitivity of the subject);
- organise material coherently (e.g. use paragraphs, headings, sub-headings, indentation and highlighting, link information and ideas in an ordered way using words such as 'however', 'therefore');
- make meaning clear by writing, proof-reading and re-drafting documents so that spelling, punctuation and grammar are accurate.

Part B

WHAT YOU MUST DO

You must:	Evidence must show you can:

C3.1a
Contribute to a group discussion about a complex subject.

- make clear and relevant contributions in a way that suits your purpose and situation;
- listen and respond sensitively to others, and develop points and ideas; and
- create opportunities for others to contribute when appropriate.

C3.1b
Make a presentation about a complex subject, using at least **one** image to illustrate complex points.

- speak clearly and adapt your style of presentation to suit your purpose, subject, audience and situation;
- structure what you say so that the sequence of information and ideas may be easily followed; and
- use a range of techniques to engage the audience, including effective use of images.

C3.2
Read and synthesise information from **two** extended documents about a complex subject.
  One of these documents should include at least **one** image.

- select and read material that contains the information you need;
- identify accurately, and compare, the lines of reasoning and main points from texts and images; and
- synthesise the key information in a form that is relevant to your purpose.

C3.3
Write **two** different types of documents about complex subjects.
  One piece of writing should be an extended document and include at least **one** image.

- select and use a form and style of writing that is appropriate to your purpose and complex subject matter;
- organise relevant information clearly and coherently, using specialist vocabulary when appropriate; and
- ensure your text is legible and your spelling, grammar and punctuation are accurate, so your meaning is clear.

To help you check whether level 3 is the best one for you to work at, try to answer the questions below, as honestly as you can, by ticking the boxes. Ask your teacher/supervisor for help if you need it.

Initial Self-assessment for Communication Level 3

Discussions

Can you:

Vary what you say, and the way that you say it, to present an argument, or to express ideas or opinions?
○ YES   ○ NO

Show that you are listening, and respond to other people in a sensitive way, which acknowledges their point of view?
○ YES   ○ NO

Give others the opportunity to contribute, by inviting them to speak, or asking suitable questions?
○ YES   ○ NO

Give an example of a discussion you have taken part in, within the last six months:

Topic:

Who took part:

The reason for the discussion:

Making a presentation

Can you:

Research material to use in the presentation, and organise it in a coherent way?
○ YES   ○ NO

Structure your presentation, so that the audience can follow your line of reasoning?
○ YES   ○ NO

Use techniques which will engage your audience by:

Giving examples which the audience can relate to?   ○ YES   ○ NO

Varying the tone of your voice?   ○ YES   ○ NO

Using images such as graphs, pictures and models to illustrate points?
○ YES   ○ NO

Give an example of a presentation you have given in the last six months:

Topic:

Audience:

Reason for the talk:

Reading

Can you:

Skim and scan extended documents, at least three pages long, to pick out the main points, and the writer's opinions and arguments?
◯YES   ◯ NO

Use appropriate sources of reference, including texts, databases, and the views of others, to clarify your argument or position?
◯YES   ◯ NO

Compare the views of others, and recognise opinion and bias?
◯YES   ◯ NO

Synthesise information by presenting your own interpretation of the topic or subject?
◯YES   ◯ NO

Give an example of reading and synthesising information that you have carried out in the last six months:

Topic:

The reason for your research:

The type of record you kept of your findings e.g. notes, report, summary, essay.

Writing

Can you:

Choose when to present information as the following types of document:

Extended essay? ◯YES   ◯ NO

Report? ◯YES   ◯ NO

Memo/Note? ◯YES   ◯ NO

Make sure that the style of your writing is suitably formal, with the right tone and level of complexity?
◯YES   ◯ NO

Make your written work clear and well organised by:

Spelling all words accurately? ◯YES   ◯ NO

Writing complex sentences correctly, with accurate punctuation?
○ YES   ○ NO

Using paragraphs, headings, sub-headings, indentations and highlighting?
○ YES   ○ NO

Give examples of two extended documents, which you have written in the last six months:

Topic:	1.	
	2.	
Type of document:	1.	
	2.	
Reason for writing it:	1.	
	2.	

What the Self-assessment shows you

If you have answered 'YES' to most or all of the questions, and have been able to give examples in each case, you should be able to achieve Communication at level 3.

 Check this with your teacher/supervisor.
If you have answered 'YES' to some of the questions, but there are gaps in your skills and knowledge, this may be the most suitable level for you.

 Check this with your teacher/supervisor.
If you have answered 'NO' to most or all of the questions, you may not be ready to tackle this level of Communication. You may need to start at level 1, or 2. Try the self-assessment at levels 1 and 2 to find out.

In order to achieve Communication at Level 3 you will need to:

- Make sure that you can do all the points in Part A.
- Practise and prepare for the test.
- Pass the test at level 3 (external assessment, set and marked by the Awarding Body).
- Collect a portfolio of evidence, which is well organised, and which shows you can do all of Part B of the unit.

- Have your portfolio assessed and checked as having enough evidence at the right standard (internal assessment, carried out by your teacher/supervisor, and checked by the Awarding Body).

Summary of Communication level 3

This Key Skills unit is equivalent to NVQ 3, Advanced GNVQ, or GCE AS/A grades A–E.

Speaking, listening, reading and writing skills are needed for complex activities, involving sensitive issues, and using extended documents.

Assessment:

External test: set and marked by Awarding Body

→ Test is one-and-a-half hours long
→ Questions are both short-answer and allowing extended writing
→ Based on Part A and Part B

■ NOTE: You may be exempt from the test if you have already achieved GCE grades A–E at AS or A level within the last three years.

Internal portfolio assessed within your school/college/ centre:

- Must cover all of Part B
- Must meet the standard
- Must be well organised

Summary of the chapter

You should now be ready to start using this book to help you achieve the Communication unit.

→ You will know which level to use in the next section of the book.
→ You will have an idea of the gaps in your skills and knowledge, which you need to develop.
→ You know how you will be assessed at each level.

Before you begin, write down any qualifications you have, any exemptions or proxies you want to claim and any other courses you are taking now:

Name of Qualifications	Grade	Date Achieved:
Exemption/proxy claimed for Communication test (tick the box):		
GCSE Grade D–G	Date	Exemption claimed ☐
A*–C		☐
GCE AS Grade A–E	Date	Exemption claimed ☐
GCE A Grade A–E	Date	Exemption claimed ☐
Name of Qualifications being taken now:	Date started:	Date of finish:

3

Communication Level 1: Developing the Skills and Knowledge in Part A

Introduction

This part of the book will help you to develop and practise your Communication skills as set out in Part A of the unit at level 1. It will also help you get ready for the test at level 1, which is based on Part A.

When speaking, listening, reading and writing, it is important to think about:

What you want to say:

What are the important facts, opinions, or points, which you want to make clear? Are you trying to explain or describe something?

Why you want to say it:

What is the reason for speaking, reading or writing and what do you intend to achieve? Are you discussing something? Do you want to argue a point of view? Are you giving information?

Who you are speaking or writing to:

How will you know that your style and approach is appropriate? Is it formal enough? What is the setting? How many people are in your audience?

Discussions (Speaking and Listening)

When preparing for a discussion:

- Know the topic.
- Know the purpose.
- Know your own role.
- Make notes.
- Try to think of some questions that you could ask others. The questions should be helpful and positive.

When taking part in any discussion:

- Make sure that you understand the reason for the discussion.
- The role of those taking part.
- Know who is leading the discussion.
- Speak clearly, using words everyone can understand.
- Make relevant points, give specific examples of what you mean.

- Ask suitable questions: try to ask an open question, which allows others to respond.
- Show by your body language that you are listening.
- Listen for the tone of people's voices.
- Watch their gestures.

Go through the checklists:

- Be prepared.
- Know who you are speaking to, and when.
- Know how long you have.
- Take part.
- Listen carefully to the tutor. She may give you specific points, which you can act on.
- If she does not give you specific advice, ask questions, such as, 'How can I get help with this part of Science?'
- Stick to the facts, say which parts of Maths you find difficult e.g. 'I find fractions very hard to do'.
- You may have to accept some criticism in this situation, perhaps your tutor will say, 'You may need to work harder on your Maths assignments, if you want to improve'.
- Write notes if you need to.
- Agree what is to be done, by you and others, and by when e.g. 'So I need to speak to Mrs Jacobs this week, to ask for extra help with fractions?'

Example:

You are reviewing your progress on your GCSE courses with your tutor in a one-to-one discussion. Perhaps you did not do as well as you expected in Maths and Science in the end-of-term review. You want to explain why and ask for more help.

Example: In your discussion with your tutor, you know that she will discuss the results of your end-of-year tests, and the effort grades you have achieved. In most subjects your test results and grades are good. You hope to receive praise for this. You also know that your results in Maths and Science are not good, and that you have not been trying very hard. You want to make clear to her that you need more help in Maths and Science, and that you are not very keen on these subjects, because you do not find them easy. There are some specific areas where you know that you need extra help. You have been able to work out which areas from your test results.

How do you prepare for, and take part in, this discussion?

Help desk

Example preparation and notes, which could be used for the above discussion:

Prepare by reading your:
→ subject reports
→ test results
→ comments on recent homework
→ feedback from tutors
→ improvements you have made

Make notes of:
→ subject grades for achievement and effort
→ test results
→ areas which your tutors have pointed out as needing improvement
→ areas which you think you need help with in maths and science
→ reasons why you have not done well in maths and science
→ ideas you have of ways to improve

Say these points during the discussion:
→ 'I did get these good grades for effort'
→ 'I don't find maths or science very easy'
→ 'I would like to get help with fractions, and how to write up experiments'
→ 'I am pleased with my results in my other subjects'
→ 'I think I have tried hard in English and humanities'

Help desk

Open Questions

These allow other people to give their own opinion, and are valuable during discussions, because they move things forward. Open questions develop ideas and allow others to join in e.g. 'What do you think about...?', 'Why do you think that happened?'

Closed Questions

Usually need 'Yes' or 'No' answers, or one-word replies:

e.g. 'What day is it today?', 'Do you want to go to the cinema?'

They are not very helpful in discussions, as they do not encourage people to give their own view or opinion.

In summary: Some Do's and Don'ts.

DO'S ✓

Choose a topic you are interested in, and know something about, if you have a choice.

Find out about the topic.

Make notes of the points you want to make.

Speak clearly, using suitable language.

Listen to others, and show you are listening. Look them in the eye.

Ask at least one relevant open question. You could ask someone to make their point more clearly.

DON'TS ✗

Be unprepared.

Use slang or jargon.

Be unclear.

Be too loud, or too quiet.

Be unsympathetic to what others say.

Ignore others.

Interrupt the person speaking.

Reading

Checklist: When getting advice on what to read:

- Make sure you are given a clear list of sources, which includes chapter or page references.
- Make sure that you understand exactly what information you need to find.
- Use the contents page and the index, to get the best from your book, CD-ROM, or other source.
- Look for key words.
- Make sure that you know what you have to do with the information.

Checklist: When trying to understand information:

- Use a dictionary for any new words.
- Ask your teacher/supervisor to explain anything you do not understand.

Checklist: When picking out the main points, and making notes:

- Pick out the key words, and write them down.
- Write down the meaning of the words.
- Put your points in a sensible order, then number them.
- Pick out a chart, picture, diagram or sketch to make a point.

Checklist: Using a dictionary:

- Words are listed in dictionaries in alphabetical order.
- The word is shown in bold.
- Then there is a letter, which tells you what type of word it is.
- Then there are explanations of the word's meaning(s).
- There are also abbreviations, and examples of use of the word, followed by the origin of the word.

Help desk

friend

Type of word = n = noun
Meanings = 1. a person well
known to another and regarded
with liking, affection, and loyalty;
an intimate. 2. an acquaintance or
associate. 3. an ally in a fight or
cause; supporter....
Uses = 6. be friends (with). 7.
make friends (with)
Origin = Old English *freond*...

ACTIVITY

You have been asked to write a magazine article on your favourite band or singer. The instructions you have been given say:

→ You should use no more than three sources of information.
→ The article must be less than one side of A4.
→ You have one week to complete the work.

You also know that you have to provide the following information, about the singer, or band:

→ Name(s)
→ Age(s)
→ Picture
→ Place(s) born
→ Brothers and sisters
→ Job(s) before becoming a singer/musician?
→ Names of chart singles and albums?
→ Place now living?
→ Boyfriend/girlfriend?
→ Future plans?
→ One other piece of information about them.

How do you read and obtain the information you need to write this article? See the helpdesk for one possible way of approaching the activity.

Go through the checklist

● Make sure that you understand the instructions.
● Ask for help if you do not.
● Find the three sources of information.
● Use the instruction list, to find all the information set out above.
● Write down the points you need to find out.
● Match the points to the list above.
● Choose a picture to include in your article.

Example notes from reading, to use when writing magazine article:

(Help) desk

Three sources used:

Teenage Dream magazine.

The Daily Enquirer newspaper.

The Cosmic Dreamtime Review.

Information noted:

Name: Cosmic Dreamtime

People in it are: Diana (vocals), Tim NB Dim (base), Rufus (drums), Jamie O (lead guitar).

Ages (in same order as above): 19, 20, 20, 18.

Picture is from 'The Cosmic Dreamtime Review' showing them in concert.

Brothers and Sisters: Diana, none; Tim, one brother and one sister; Rufus, one brother; Jamie, one sister.

Previous jobs: Diana, waitress; Tim, toilet attendant; Rufus, taxi driver; Jamie, cook in a greasy Joe café.

Chart singles: Universe and now Love lost.

Albums: *Cosmic Dreamtime Catches Light* is their debut.

Living: All live in London.

Boy/girl friends: Diana and Rufus are an item, Tim is going out with Sheila from the TV series *Westend*, Jamie is between relationships.

Future plans and other information: to make another album. Diana wants to buy a château in France, Rufus is saving for a new drum kit and wants to rescue greyhounds. Tim wants to invest in a chain of designer public toilets, and Jamie wants to play with Eric Clapton. After the singing days are over he wants to learn to cook properly and open a smart restaurant somewhere.

Plan the article, use headings, decide where to put picture. Write in rough and check.

Re-write final version.

In summary: some Do's and Don'ts.

DO'S ✓

Get help from your teacher/supervisor about what to read.

Make sure you are clear about what information you are looking for.

Ask for help if you are not clear about what you have read.

Make notes which will help you.

Choose useful pictures, charts or diagrams.

DON'TS X

Start reading without a clear picture of what you want to know.

Be afraid to ask questions, if you need to.

Write things which you do not understand.

Make notes which are too long.

Choose too many images.

Writing

Checklist: When writing:

Make sure that you know the layout for:

A memo:

This is a way of giving information or instructions to one or more people in a formal work situation, or to record what has happened.

- Put the heading 'Memo' or 'Memorandum' in large letters at the top.
- Say who it is to.
- Give the name(s) of anyone else to whom the memo is to be circulated as Copy Circulated (CC).
- Say who it is from.
- Give the date.
- State the subject of the memo.
- Make the memo short and to the point.
- Write in note form.

Example:

(**Help**) *desk*)

Memo

To: Dave, Linda, Diane, Susan, Rajiv
CC: Mrs Singh
From: Sarah
4 Feb 2001

The school play

This is to confirm that the final rehearsal is tomorrow night, 5 Feb, 4.15–6.15 in the school hall. Please make sure that everyone brings their costume and props. There will be drinks and sandwiches during the rehearsal.
If you need to know anything else, please get in touch.
Thank you,

Sarah

A business letter:

This is an example of a formal letter.

- Write this type of letter when applying for a job or grant, when writing to any organisation, including Government offices, making a complaint, requesting information or payment.
- Put your name and address in the top right-hand corner.
- Put the name and address of the person you are writing to underneath, but on the left side of the page.
- Put the date underneath.

- Below the date start the letter with: 'Dear Sir', 'Dear Madam' or 'Dear Ms Brown'.
- Use formal language, explaining clearly why you are writing.
- End the letter with 'Yours faithfully' if it started 'Dear Sir or Madam', or 'Yours sincerely' if it started with 'Dear Ms Brown'.
- Sign, and print your name underneath.

Example:

Help desk

Steven Chan
1 The Pines
Woodley
Leafdale
Surrey
SV1 2UU

Mr Strange
Savalot Supermarket
Severnack
Surrey
SV2 2VV

10 January 2001

Dear Mr Strange,

I am writing to ask for details of the Saturday job, advertised in the Severnack Times on 8 January. Please send me an application form for the job, as I am very keen to obtain a part-time job in the local area. I have some experience of working in a shop, which I enjoyed, and I would like the opportunity to do this in a larger store such as yours.

I look forward to hearing from you,

Yours sincerely,

Steven Chan

A report:

This is an account of an event. You have to:

- Describe what has happened.
- Explain where it happened.
- Say why it happened.
- State who was part of the event.
- Use a heading and sub-headings.
- Make points, use bullets or numbers where sensible.

Example:

Help desk

Super School Sports Day

The events

The Super School Sports Day on 15 July was well attended by parents and Governors of the school. Every form in the lower school entered the relay competitions. For the first time swimming races were held in the newly built pool. The parent combined sack race and the egg and spoon had its biggest entry ever, and certainly raised the loudest cheers of the day.

The winners

Prizes and cups were presented by the Chair of Governors, Samantha Devas, and local councillor Reginald Straws gave the shield for best House to Hanover, and for individual achievement to Jeremy Redfurn. In the swimming pool Susannah De Faux took the honours.

Next year

Next year the day is planned to coincide with the school's 25th anniversary celebrations, and promises to be bigger and better than ever.

A short essay:

This is one way to answer a question, to write an assignment, or perhaps a piece of coursework.

- The most important thing is to answer the question.
- Plan your essay, so that it has a beginning, a middle, and an end.
- Write a rough draft after your plan.
- The rough draft has key points, key words, your basic ideas, and the order of your essay.
- Write clearly, in sentences.
- Use paragraphs to divide the essay into sections; beginning, middle and end.

Example:

Help desk

The Life of Charles Darwin

Charles Darwin was born in Shrewsbury on 12 February 1809. His father was a doctor. He wanted Charles to be a doctor. His mother died when he was eight years old.

Charles Darwin went to school in Shrewsbury. He did not do well at school. He did not want to be a doctor. He was more interested in collecting animals and shells. Darwin went to university at Cambridge, where he studied to be a church man. He did not work very hard though.

He would have been a vicar if two of his friends had not asked him to go to South America. They asked him to sail to South America on HMS Beagle. At first he said no. Later he changed his mind and sailed on the Beagle on 27 December 1831. He was very seasick.

He travelled round South America and collected fossils and plants and animals. Then he sailed to some islands in the Pacific Ocean called Galapagos. Darwin got his ideas for his theory of evolution from watching the animals there.

When he came home he got married to Emma and had children. He moved to Kent and wrote books. He sorted out all the fossils, plants and animals he had collected.

He enjoyed himself a lot playing games with his children. He was quite ill and as he got older he got worse. Darwin died in his sleep on 19 April 1882. He is buried in Westminster Abbey with other famous people.

An application form:

- Write in capitals or type, so that your words are very clear.
- Give the facts about yourself, and your experience.
- Do not make things up.
- Be as positive as you can about the things you can do.

Example:

Help desk

Savalot Supermarket
Application form

Complete this form in block capitals:

Last name:

First names:

Address:

Telephone number:

Date of birth:

Names and addresses of schools/colleges attended since age 11:

Dates:

From:

To:

Examinations taken or about to be taken:

GCSE:

Grade:

Date:

AS/A:

Grade:

Date:

GNVQ:

Level:

Grade:

Date:

List any other courses and qualifications taken or about to be taken.

Give details of any work experience or part-time work you have had.

Interests and activities including voluntary work, clubs, hobbies and sport. This could include activities inside or outside school.

Give details of any special achievements or positions of responsibility, such as prefect, Duke of Edinburgh Award, etc.

Please say why you are interested in this post, and why you consider yourself suitable.

Signature:

Date:

Use a picture, chart, diagram or sketch to make a point:

(Help) desk

The unusual shape of the Sydney opera house:

The exhilaration of being first in a race.

This diagram of the eye shows the main tissues it contains.

The rough sketch shows how the units could be fitted into the kitchen.

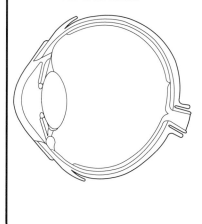

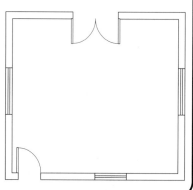

Use only helpful information, and write a sensible amount to:

- Ask for information.
- Give information.
- Give your opinion.
- Make suggestions.
- Express your ideas.

Proofread your work and change, if necessary, to make sure that you have:

Spelt everyday words correctly by:
- Identifying and circling new words.
- Checking the spelling is correct.
- Keeping a spelling book, with a list of words.
- Adding new words to your list.
- Practising your spelling every day.
- Covering the word, trying to spell it, checking your spelling.

Help desk

Examples of words you should be able to spell, but which are easily misspelled:

there	their	they're	thieve
belief	believe	receive	achieve
choose	chose	choice	cheque
which	witch	whole	where
height	weight	weird	were
leisure	pleasure	acquire	accurate
seize	size	says	science
weather	whether	Wednesday	wear

Follow the basic rules of grammar, to put words into the correct order, and to make sure:
- The verb agrees with the subject.
- The tense is used consistently.

Examples:
She **was** very pleased with the gift.
Not: She **were** very pleased with the gift.

The people **were** going to the game.
Not: They **was** going to the game.

Use correct punctuation:
- Punctuation is used to put a pause or space between words.
- This helps to make more sense of the words, and to give emphasis, when speaking or reading.

- You should be able to use capital letters, full stops and question marks.

Examples:

The tortoise ate some dandelions.

What did the rabbit eat?

She worked for Sky T.V.

J.F.K. was the president of the U.S.A.

Help desk

Type of word:	How it is used:
Verb	A verb is used to describe an action.
	Examples: to run, to play, to hide, to laugh, to fight, to talk, to write.
	Verbs change depending on the tense, which tells you if the action happened in the past, is happening now, or will happen in the future.
	The form of the verb must agree with the subject.
	Examples: She did play with the dog. We fed the cat.
Noun	A noun is the name of a person, a place, an animal, plant or thing.
	Examples: Peter, Peterborough, panther, primrose, pencil.
	The names of people, places, organisations, days, months and seasons are given capital letters.
Adjective	An adjective describes a noun or a pronoun.
	Examples: large, small, bad, yellow.
Adverb	An adverb describes a verb or an adjective.
	Examples: quickly, sadly, good, badly.
Pronoun	A pronoun is used instead of a noun.
	Examples: she, he, it.

Help desk

Tense: The tense tells you if the action happened in the past, is happening now, or will happen in the future. These are the past, present and future tenses.

In summary. Some Do's and Don'ts.

DO'S ✓

Use a suitable style of writing.

Follow the rules for different types of writing.

Plan and structure reports and essays.

Use pictures, charts and diagrams to make your points more clearly.

Proofread and change if needed.

DON'TS ✗

Wander away from the point or the question.

Spell words wrongly.

Use wrong punctuation.

Ignore the rules of grammar.

DEFINITIONS ▶

Key Skills Words: Teacher/supervisor/assessor:

All or some of these people could be helping you to develop your Communication skills. The name will depend on whether you are in a school, college, working with a training provider, an NVQ student or modern apprentice. In this book, the person who helps you will be your assessor. This person will decide if your evidence meets the standards set out in the unit.

4

Communication Level 1: Practice Test Questions on Part A

Introduction

Now that you have developed and practised the Communication Skills set out in Part A of the unit, you are ready to try some short multiple-choice questions. If you find any of these questions difficult, go back to Chapter 3 for more help before moving on in the book.

Here are some short answer questions to check that you have all the skills and knowledge as set out in Part A. These are followed by some example multiple-choice questions, showing the type of questions seen in the external tests. The external test will not have questions on discussions.

Short answer questions

Discussions (Speaking and Listening)

ACTIVITY

Prepare for and take part in a discussion with two or three people about your most recent work experience, or your part-time job. Each person should share their experience and compare it with others in the group.

1. Make notes to include the following:
- Name and address of employer.
- Health and safety rules.
- Employer's business e.g. type of business, size, number of staff, how long it has existed, local or national, staff facilities.
- Your job, and what is expected of you.
- Rate of pay (if known).
- A day in your life at work.
- How long you worked there.
- Your hours.
- Your journey there and back.
- What you liked about it.
- What you didn't like about it.
- Is this the type of work you would like to do when you leave school/college?

2. Take part in the discussion. Try to contribute as much as you can from your notes, without interrupting others.

3. Now fill in the evaluation about the discussion below. Try to be as honest as possible.

Use your evaluation to improve on future discussions, such as those suggested in parts 2 and 3 of this book.

Self Evaluation:

When I spoke I made the following points:

I listened to these people speak:

I answered these questions:

Did you interrupt anyone?   Yes ☐   No ☐

I asked these questions:

Something I liked about the discussion:

Turn to page 50 for discussion on this activity.

Reading:

ACTIVITY

The following piece of writing is about children's safety when riding micro-scooters. Pick out the main points from the article which parents should know about, to help their children to be safer when using them. (Taken from *Sunday Mirror*, 8 October 2000):

Last night parents were urged to make their children wear crash helmets on micro-scooters. As this latest designer craze has seen a 700% increase in accidents, in the past four months, parents are being warned to buy their children safety gear when they purchase a scooter. The Royal Society for the Prevention of Accidents (RoSPA) is about to issue safety guidance for the scooters.

There are thousands being sold each week, and there has already been one death. Nine-year-old Aaron Jenkins died when he collided with a taxi, whilst riding his scooter. As the scooters only cost £100 and are popular with children, adults, and even stars such as Robbie Williams and Gail Porter, many more accidents are just waiting to happen. Children should not be using them on or near busy main roads.

The most common types of injury are broken and dislocated arms and legs, but more serious head injuries are also a worry. The guidance from RoSPA will include essential safety equipment including crash helmets, and elbow and knee guards. Micro-scooters are going to be top of most children's Christmas list, and with darker evenings coming, there may be an increase in the number of accidents. Many young riders do not use reflectors or lights to be easily seen, and would be best advised not to ride at night. RoSPA wants people to use micro-scooters safely, not spoil their fun.

Turn to page 51 for an example list of safety points.

ACTIVITY

The following images are all about types of love and relationships. Underneath the pictures there is a set of statements. Match each statement to a picture:

Pictures A–F

Statements 1–6

1. Puppy love
2. The romance is over
3. The marriage is over
4. True friends
5. Romance blooms
6. Wedding bells chime

Turn to page 51 for the correct matches.

Writing

ACTIVITY

Spot the spelling errors in the following paragraph:
Cycling Today
Peeple who cycle in compatitions now ware equipment,
which helps them to travell faster. They have teardrop
shaped helmets and skinsuits to cut down wind resistence.
The bycycles used have much liter weels, tyres and frames.
The rider now crowches low over the bike, to allow faster,
stronger peadalling. Solid-disc weels lower the wind drag as
they spin. All of this meens that modern cyclists brake
speed records all the time.

Turn to page 51 for the correctly spelt version.

ACTIVITY

Improve the grammar and punctuation in the following
paragraph:

Ken Hom
Ken hom is a well known chef on TV he was born in
America in 1949 growing up in chicagos chinatown learning
English and not finding school easy but his uncles
restaurant is where working at weekends he starts his
cooking? Kens chinese cooking is what makes him a
famous chef world known for his leading new
developments into the future for cooking.

Turn to page 52 for the correctly punctuated version,
with improved sentence structure.

Short answer questions for pages 47–50:

Discussions (Speaking and Listening)

You should have been able to contribute about half of the
points in the list. In your evaluation you should have noted

who else spoke to you, and any questions you answered or asked. You should not have interrupted anyone.

If you are not happy with your performance in the discussion, go back to Chapter 3, use the checklists and Help Desks, then try again. Remember this part of the book is to help you develop and practise your skills. It is very likely that you will need to take part in more than one discussion before you are ready to be observed and assessed.

Reading

The main points you should have listed about safety for children using micro-scooters are:

Guidance for parents who buy their children micro-scooters:
- Buy safety equipment for your child.
- This should include a crash helmet, elbow and knee guards.
- Do not allow your child to ride on or near busy main roads.
- Do not use the scooter at night, and definitely not without lights and reflectors.

If you have missed any points, you may need to read more carefully. Look for key words, such as: safety, equipment, helmet, lights.

If you have written much more than this, you need to practise choosing only the points asked for. In this case only information for parents was needed.

Use the Checklists and Help Desk in Chapter 3, for more guidance. Don't worry about having another go at this before you are ready to be assessed.

Correct matches of the pictures to the statements:

A 5	B 1	C 6
D 3	E 4	F 2

If you have got any of these wrong, use the checklists and help desk in Chapter 3. Remember the pictures must show the best image for that phrase or sentence.

Writing

Cycling today

People who cycle in competitions now wear equipment, which helps them to travel faster. They have teardrop shaped helmets and skinsuits to cut down wind resistance. The bicycles used have much lighter wheels, tyres and frames. The rider now crouches low over the bike, to allow faster, stronger pedalling. Solid-disc wheels lower the drag as they spin. All of this means that modern cyclists break speed records all the time.

The corrected words are listed below:

people	competitions	wear
travel	resistance	bicycles
lighter	wheels	crouches
pedalling	means	break

If you spelt some words wrongly, go back to the Checklists and the Help Desks on in Chapter 3. Practise your spelling of everyday words more regularly.

Ken Hom

Ken Hom is a well known T.V. chef. He was born in America in 1949. He grew up in Chicago's Chinatown. This is where he learned English. He did not find school easy. He started cooking in his uncle's restaurant, working there at weekends. Ken's Chinese cooking has made him a world famous chef. He leads new developments in cooking.

If you could not improve the punctuation and grammar, go back to the Checklists and the Help Desks in Chapter 3.

Multiple-choice questions

Now try these multiple-choice questions, which will test your Communication skills in the same way as the one-hour external assessment. Dictionaries are not allowed in the test. You will have 60 minutes to answer 40 questions.

In each case the question is followed by four possible answers. Only one of these is the right answer. Choose the word, sentence, or phrase, which you think is correct, and write down the letter which matches it. This is your answer.

Example:
The waiter was asked to return all the wine glasses to .... correct place on the shelf.
Choose the correct word to fill the gap above

A there	B they're
C their	D th'ere

If you think the answer is 'their' put the letter C. (This is the correct answer.)

The answers to the following 12 example questions can be found on page 55. Try to answer the questions yourself, before you check them. You will have to answer 40 questions in one hour in the text.

Questions 1–4 are based on the letter below.

Rock View

12 Stony Avenue

Granite

Wessex

GG51 3QZ

12 December 2000

Dear Mr Hemingway,

I am _____(A) to apply for the post of office assistant in your publishing company. As requested in your _____(B) in the South East Chronicle, I am also sending my C.V. I have included the two _____(C) you asked for.

I would be able to come to your offices for an interview on the following dates:

15–19 December

22–24 December

Yours _____(D)

John Agius

---

1. The spelling at (A) should be:

A writing   B writeing
C righting   D wrighteing

2. The spelling at (B) should be:

A advetisement   B advetisemont
C advertissement   D advertissment

3. The spelling at (C) should be:

A refarences   B references
C refferences   D refarencis

4. At (D) the letter should end:

A faithfully   B truly
C gratefully   D sincerely

5. Sarah is going to apply for a job. What type of document should she write?

A Memo

B Essay

C Letter

D Notes

Questions 6–8 are based on the poster below

Day Trips to France Through the Channel Tunnel

A quick, easy day out with *Caring Coaches* for only £28.00 adults, £20.00 children.

Family ticket £82.00 (up to 2 adults + up to 3 children).

Price includes coach and tunnel fare, with 5 hours in Calais for Xmas Shopping.

All coaches fitted with seat belts, toilets and drinks machine.

Departure dates: 15, 16, 17 December

Departure times: 7.00 a.m. from Town Square, 7.20 a.m. from The Chequers, 7.30 a.m. from Hanson's Corner

Book now on: 011113 454647

---

6. Which of the following is an opinion?

A Price includes coach fare

B 5 hours in Calais

C All coaches fitted with seat belts

D A quick, easy day out

7. The cost for a family of two adults and two children would be:

A £96.00

B £82.00

C £116.00

D £80.00

8. The poster provides people with:

A Costs, dates and times of the day trips

B Details of Channel Tunnel costs

C Interesting facts about Calais

D Details of the journey

9. David is going to visit a friend who has recently moved to a new area. David's friend should send him a:

A Map of the town he now lives in

B Picture of his new house

C Chart of house prices in his new town

D Plan of his new house

10. Which of the following sentences is punctuated correctly?

A Why didn't you buy the phone.

B Did you want to buy the phone.

C He did not have enough money to buy the phone.

D The phone is not worth the money?

11. We're could also be written

A we'er   B were

C wer'e   D we are

12. Another word for spacious is

A small   B large

C busy   D loud

The answers to questions 1-12 on page 52:

1. A	2. C	3. B
4. D	5. C	6. D
7. B	8. A	9. A
10. C	11. D	12. B

If you got some answers wrong, you need to practise:

Questions 1–3 Spelling

Questions 4–5 Formats of documents

Questions 6–8 Reading and finding information

Question 9 Using images

Questions 10–12 Understanding the meaning of words and sentences

Communication Level 1: Activities for Practice (Part A) or Assessment (Part B)

Introduction

This part of the book will help you to check that you have developed all the skills, and have all the knowledge set out, in Part A of the Communication unit. You will then be ready to use these skills in assignments, tasks and everyday situations in work, school or college, to produce evidence for your portfolio.

In this section you will also start to get ideas for activities and tasks, which you can use as evidence in your portfolio. This is needed to meet Part B of the unit.

When you have practised your skills, you will be ready to plan activities and assignments, to apply your skills, and to show what you can do in your portfolio of evidence. Whether you use the activities and tasks here, to continue to develop your skills, OR you use them in your portfolio for assessment is up to you. There are record sheets in this chapter for Part A, if you are still practising your skills. There are also tracking and recording sheets in this chapter if you are ready to be assessed on your evidence.

Copy the following sheet to keep an on-going record of your developing skills and knowledge. Use it to record examples of tasks and assignments, which have helped you practise your skills. You may only need one example here, or you may need more than two, depending upon your skill level when you start this unit.

Communication Part A	One example of an activity which has helped me develop and practise my skills is:	One example of an activity which has helped me develop and practise my skills is:
1.1 Discussions Find information Make useful points Speak clearly Listen carefully Ask questions		
1.2 Reading Get advice Check understanding Pick out main points Make notes Use a dictionary		
1.3 Writing Write: Letter Memo Notes Report Essay Application form Use images Choose how much to write Proofread, and change Use correct: Spelling Grammar Punctuation		

1.1 Discussions

You could use any example of a discussion, but if you want to use the evidence in your portfolio, someone needs to observe you and record your skills and evidence, as having met the criteria as shown below. You will need to be supervised for this to take place and for your assessor to confirm your skills. You could use a video or audio tape as part of your evidence. You can help this process by keeping your own records of the discussion using the tracking and recording sheets like those which follow on pages 59 and 60. These sheets can be used to show how your skills are developing. They could also be part of your portfolio evidence, to help show that you can use your skills in different situations.

Examples of discussions you could take part in:

- The advantages and disadvantages of living away from home (Group discussion)
- Work experience and what you got out of it (Group discussion)

- Your pet, and how you look after it (Group discussion)
- What you watch on T.V. (Group discussion)
- A book or play that you have read (Group discussion)
- Careers interview with a careers advisor (One-to-one discussion)
- A part-time/full-time job interview (One-to-one)
- Tell another person about your most recent holiday (One-to-one)
- Tell another person about your work experience (One-to-one)
- Tell another person who your favourite famous person is, and why (One-to-one)
- Tell another person about something you did well on your work placement/experience (One-to-one)

Example:

A Part-time/Full-time Job Interview

Preparation for a job interview: Trainee in an estate agents
Read:
→ the job advertisement again
→ the job description again
→ your own application form and/or letter
→ any other information sent to you

Pick out:
→ the types of activities you would have to do each day
→ qualifications needed
→ the personal skills needed
→ experiences that would be useful

Make notes of:
→ Useful experiences e.g. worked in an office before
→ Your ability to do the job e.g. any feedback from work experience or previous jobs
→ Any examples of achievements in the workplace
→ Why you think you would like the job e.g. you enjoy working with people, you are well organised at paper work
→ Some questions to ask e.g. would there be training/career opportunities?

Taking part in a job interview: Trainee in an estate agents
→ Dress appropriately for the interview
→ Sit comfortably without slumping in the chair
→ Listen carefully to what you are being asked
→ Look at the interviewer
→ Answer the questions clearly
→ Smile and look interested in what they say

Note: This could be a real interview or a practice/mock interview

Communication Part B Tracking and Recording Sheets

Tracking and Recording sheets

Communication Level 1 Part B	Evidence must show you can:
C1.1 Discussions Take part in a one-to-one discussion about a straightforward subject	• Provide information that is relevant to the subject and purpose of the discussion • Speak clearly in a way that suits the situation • Listen and respond appropriately to what others say

I took part in a discussion with:

Date of the discussion:

The discussion was about:

The purpose of the discussion was:

I spoke clearly to make these points:

1
2
3

I listened to these points:

1
2
3

I asked these questions:

1
2
3

Tracking and Recording sheets

Communication Level 1 Part B **C1.1 Discussions** Take part in a group discussion about a straightforward subject.	**Evidence must show you can:** • Provide information that is relevant to the subject and purpose of the discussion. • Speak clearly in a way that suits the situation. • Listen and respond appropriately to what others say.
I took part in a discussion with these people: Date of the discussion: The discussion was about: The purpose of the discussion was:	They are people: I know/do not know
I spoke clearly to these people to make these points:	1st Person: Point: 2nd Person: Point: 3rd Person: Point:
I listened to these points, made by these people:	1st Person: Point: 2nd Person: Point: 3rd Person: Point:
I asked these questions, to these people:	1st Person: Question: 2nd Person: Question: 3rd person: Question:

Summary: Some common problems and solutions:

Summary

Problem	Solution
Not enough preparation.	Be very clear about the topic.
	Take enough time.
	Make good notes.
Speaking too much, gabbling or rushing.	Practise what you want to say *before* the discussion.
	Do not interrupt.
Speaking too little.	Decide on one or two points that you will make.
	Practise what you want to say *before* the discussion.
Not listening to others.	It's easy to think that you have heard what someone has said, rather than what they did say.
	Focus on the speaker.
	Make notes if you need to.
	Try not to listen to what you want to hear.
Ignoring the views of others.	Do not get too excited or agitated by someone else's point of view.
	Remember – not everyone thinks the same as you.
	Try not to listen to what you want to hear.
	Do not attack people for their point of view. Don't make it personal.

If you are having lots of problems, return to step one in Chapter 3. Check your checklists, go to the Help Desks and ask for advice if you need to, *before* you go on to the next set of practice tasks and assignments.

1.2 Reading

You could use any example of materials to read, but if you want to use the evidence in your portfolio, someone needs to record your skills and evidence as having met the criteria. You can help this process by keeping your own records of your reading using tracking and recording sheets like those which follow on page 63. These sheets can be used to show how your skills are developing. They could also be part of your portfolio evidence, to help show that you can use your skills in different situations.

Examples of some topics for reading, and picking out the main points, to practise your skills:

- The religion and customs of a culture different from your own.
- A successful local business.
- A recent news issue.
- Leisure facilities available for young people in your area.
- Your rights as an employee.
- Research for a GCSE or vocational assignment.

Help desk

Key Skills Words: Purpose
Remember in each case you must have a purpose for your reading. This means that you must have a reason for reading. You must say why you need to get the information, and what you will use it for.

Example:

The Religion and Customs of Islam

Decide:
→ What you will do with the information you find e.g. write an information sheet for people of the same age as you.
→ What your sources of information will be e.g. Encarta, library book.
→ What the key words in the title of the question or assignment are e.g. 'religion' and 'customs'.
→ The main ideas and points you want to make under each key word e.g. religious festivals, beliefs, foods eaten, rules of the religion, religious places.
→ The photographs, or other images you want to use e.g. a mosque, Mecca, prayer mats.

Action:
→ Plan the layout of the information sheet.
→ Produce a draft.
→ Proofread and check your work.
→ Get feedback on your work.
→ Produce the final version.

Communication Part B Tracking and Recording Sheets

Tracking and Recording sheets

Communication Level 1 Part B
C1.2 Reading

Read and obtain information from two different types of documents, about straightforward subjects, including one image

I read and found information from at least two types of documents:

I was trying to find out about:

The main points I found:

1

2

3

The image I used was a:

I used my notes for this purpose:

Evidence must show you can:

- Read relevant materials.
- Identify accurately the main points and ideas in material.
- Use the information to suit your purpose.

Book ☐
Magazine ☐
Memo ☐
Letter ☐
Newspaper ☐
Other ☐

4

5

6

7

Picture ☐
Chart ☐
Diagram ☐

Summary: *Some common problems and solutions:*

Summary

Problem	Solution
Reading things which are not really useful.	Get a clear list from your teacher/supervisor. Stick to the list. Pick out key words and points as a list.
Choosing areas and points from your reading, which are not strictly needed.	Do not wander from your list. Understand what you are reading.
Making notes, which are vague, too long or not clear.	Make short notes. Points must be specific. Put points in order. Understand your notes. Know what your notes are for: use in a discussion, to write a report.

If you are having lots of problems, return to step one in Chapter 3. Check your checklists, go to the Help Desks and ask for advice if you need to, *before* you go on to the next set of practice tasks and assignments.

1.3 Writing

You could use any example of writing, but if you want to use the evidence in your portfolio, someone needs to record your skills and evidence as having met the criteria. You can help this process by keeping your own records of your writing using tracking and recording sheets like those which follow on page 66. These sheets can be used to show how your skills are developing. They could also be part of your portfolio evidence, to help show that you can use your skills in different situations.

Examples of some documents you could write:
- A set of instructions for finding a local building/place of interest/Youth Club/cinema.
- Report on a successful, local conservation project.
- Poster advertising a concert of your favourite band.
- An information leaflet for young people aged 16-19 about reducing the risks of HIV infection.

- A letter applying for a part-time job.
- An advertisement for a new computer game: *Sonic Spiders*.
- A poster showing how young people can get help if they are being abused.
- Questionnaire to find out how much exercise people in your organisation take.
- GCSE or vocational assignment/coursework.
- Report on a topic in the news.

Example:

Report on a news topic: Foot and Mouth disease in Essex (Spring 2001)

There are now five cases of Foot and Mouth in Essex. One of the areas belongs to the Essex Wildlife Trust. Farmers are very worried that the disease will spread around the county. One farm has had all its pigs destroyed already, and now 600 sheep may be killed as well. The farmers think that they will lose all their animals.

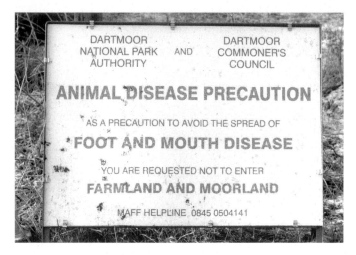

Preventing the Spread

The disease is spreading fast. No-one really knows how it is spread. This means that to try and stop it all animals must stay on their farms. All the footpaths in Essex have been closed, and the farmers' market has been stopped. Everyone is being told not to go into the countryside. Dogs must be kept on leads. Other events have been cancelled or put off. These include sponsored walks, local theatre shows and bird watching.

Communication Part B Tracking and Recording Sheets

Tracking and Recording sheets

Communication Level 1 Part B C1.3 Writing

Write two different types of document about straightforward subjects, including one image in one document.

Evidence must show you can:

- Present information in a form that suits your purpose.
- Ensure text is legible.
- Make sure that spelling, punctuation and grammar are accurate so your meaning is clear.

Document 1	Document 2
Type of document I wrote:	Type of document I wrote:
Letter ☐	Letter ☐
Memo ☐	Memo ☐
Application form ☐	Application form ☐
Notes ☐	Notes ☐
Report ☐	Report ☐
Essay ☐	Essay ☐
The image I have used is:	The image I have used is:
I wrote document 1 as .... because....................................	I wrote document 2 as .... because....................................
I have checked my work for spelling, punctuation and grammar:	I have checked my work for spelling, punctuation and grammar:
I have changed my work to make sure that it can be easily read by others, and that it is clear:	I have changed my work to make sure that it can be easily read by others, and that it is clear:
Yes ☐ No ☐	Yes ☐ No ☐

Summary: *Some common problems and solutions:*

Summary

Problem	Solution
Writing too much, and waffling.	Stick to your list of points. Write in short, clear sentences.
Not using an appropriate style.	Make sure that you understand the task or assignment set, before you begin.
Not using images sensibly.	Choose a picture, graph or chart only if it supports a point which you want to make.
Not proofreading and correcting.	Use a dictionary or spell checker. Check that the basic rules of grammar and punctuation have been applied.

If you are having lots of problems, return to step one in Chapter 3. Check your checklists, go to the Help Desks and ask for advice if you need to, *before* you go on to the next set of practice tasks and assignments.

Communication Level 1: Activities for Assessment of Part B

Portfolio Assignments Level 1

These are further examples which can be used as portfolio evidence to meet Part B of the unit requirements. Some of the examples focus on one component of Communication, others are larger, combined assignments.

In Communication you can evidence each component separately, or together.

You *should not try* to separate the criteria within each component e.g. when you take part in a discussion, you must show that you have:

Provided relevant information

AND

Spoken clearly

AND

Listened to others.

Help desk

Communication unit: Part B

Three components or parts at
level 1.

C1.1 Discussions
C1.2 Reading
C1.3 Writing

These three parts can be evidenced
separately, or together.

Each component or part has three
criteria. Example: C1.1 Discussions

• Provide information that is
  relevant to the subject and
  purpose of the discussion.

• Speak clearly in a way that suits
  the situation.

• Listen and respond appropriately
  to what others say.

These three criteria should not be separated when you produce
evidence of your discussion for your portfolio.

There are ideas below for activities, which are designed to
evidence separately:

1) Discussions

2) Reading

3) Writing

There are activities involving:

1) Reading and discussion

2) Reading and writing

There are activities involving:

Discussion, reading and writing

Ideas for activities.

1.1 Discussions

• Take part in a discussion about your favourite T.V. programme.
• Take part in a group discussion about getting help and
  information about racial harassment.
• Take part in a group discussion about the different types of
  personal bank and savings accounts available to young people.
• Take part in a group discussion about an environmental issue.
• Take part in a one-to-one discussion with someone about how
  you use your leisure time.
• You have a part-time job. The hours you work have been
  arranged around your school/college timetable and study time.

- Now your employer wants you to work more hours each week, and has said that if you cannot do this, you will be sacked. Take part in a discussion about how to deal with this situation.

1.2 Reading

- Prepare notes ready to take part in a group discussion about getting help and information about racial harassment.
- Prepare notes on the different types of personal bank and savings accounts available to young people.
- Prepare notes on how you use your leisure time.

1.3 Writing

- Write an information sheet about the different types of personal bank and savings accounts available to young people.
- Fill in an application form for a driving licence, as part of your preparation to become a driver.
- Write a letter to a close friend to cheer them up after a long stay in hospital.
- Write a memo with the following information:
  You are the Human Resources administration assistant in an electrical company. You have to inform all staff about a Health and Safety training course which everyone must attend, on 12 January from 9.30–12.30.
- Write an up to date C.V. (curriculum vitae), as part of your personal career planning and preparation for courses post-16.

(Help) desk

The term C.V. means a summary of:
Your personal details, such as name and address.
Your qualifications.
Details of your education record, such as which schools, and when, you attended.
Your other experiences, and responsibilities, such as outdoor pursuits, being a prefect, being a team captain.
Your hobbies and interests, and sporting activities.

Example CV:

Name: Joanna Duffield

Address: 21a The Crocuses, Woodland Way, Crowberry, Wilts.
WW0 1XZ

Qualifications:

GCSE grades achieved in 2000
English Language D
English Spoken 2
Mathematics E
Science E
Humanities D

GNVQ Part One
Business Pass

Education:
1995–2000, Woodlands School, Salisbury Lane, Crowberrry, Wilts.
WW6 3BQ

Responsibilities: Library assistant, school reception duties.

Additional experience:
Work experience placement for 4 weeks at local council offices, as
clerical assistant in the Planning department, in year 11.

Part-time job, for 8 hours per week, 1998–2000, in Savalot
Supermarket, Salisbury, as assistant on the delicatessen counter.

School activities: holiday to South of France, for watersports, and
canoeing in the Ardeche, Summer 1999.

Hobbies and interests:
Outdoor activities, such as windsurfing and sailing. I belong to a
local canoe club. I was a venture scout 1997–1999, and I did a
sponsored canoe, for 10 miles, to raise money for a children's
hospice in May 2000.

1.1, 1.2 Reading and discussion

- Prepare for a discussion with your supervisor/tutor about the courses you hope to take after your GCSEs. Take part in the discussion and evaluate your performance.
- Find out about the number of people in your organisation who have mobile phones, and how often they use them. Are they aware of the possible health risks of using mobile phones? Prepare notes ready to take part in a group discussion about your findings. After the discussion fill in an evaluation, like the one on page 48 in Chapter 4.
- Plan and budget for a holiday. Explain your ideas to someone else.

1.2, 1.3 Reading and writing

- Find out about the costs of living away from home, and write an information sheet for 16–19 year olds, who may want to leave home.
- Compare the costs of running a car and a motorbike. Take into account tax, insurance and fuel costs. Choose a particular make and model of car and motorbike. Write your findings in a table.
- Find out about a local business. Include information about the structure and function of the business, including production, marketing and sales. How does the business manage its own staff, customer service, and its finance? Create a display about how the business works.
- Find out about accident and emergency procedures and first aid arrangements at your place of work (full-time, part-time or work experience placement). Produce an information sheet for others to use, giving them guidelines for first aid, and accident and emergency procedures.

1.1, 1.2, 1.3 Reading, discussion and writing

- Carry out a survey of the achievements in sport/societies/clubs at your school or college. Prepare notes on your findings. Take part in a discussion about the greatest achievements of the year. Write an article about the sporting/societies/clubs achievements for a college/school newsletter or magazine.
- You are a member of your local community association, and have been asked to identify the advantages and disadvantages of the proposal to open a youth club in the town centre on Thursday, Friday and Saturday nights, from 7.00–10.00 p.m. Write a report on the matter. Discuss your ideas with someone else. Part of your report should include information on how you would get the views of other local residents regarding the youth club.

Help desk

Carrying out a survey of sporting achievements at Olympic College:

1) Plan your activity, with steps to take, and amount of time needed.
2) Identify the information you need, from the sources provided.
3) Pick out the main points e.g. which sports, competitions, teams, results will you report on?
4) Write notes on your findings e.g. as a list, or a table.
5) What points will you want to make in the discussion?
6) Which achievement do you think is the greatest?
7) What information do you want to include in the article?
8) Who is the article written for?
9) How long is the article going to be?
10) Do you need any images? If so, which ones?
11) Prepare a draft, check and correct if necessary. Produce the final version.

Communication Level 1: Putting Your Portfolio Together for Part B

Introduction

This part of the book will help you to plan your assignments, and your portfolio, to meet Part B of the Communication unit. This section also has some record sheets, to help you plan and track your progress. You can use any of the ideas and examples in the first parts of the book to provide evidence. Remember that the contexts in which you developed your skills for Part A should be different to those used to show the application of your skills for Part B. Your portfolio examples should not be re-worked or rehearsed tasks, but should show you can build on what you have learned, and that you can apply your skills in new situations.

Planning:

This is the process of:
- Taking the whole set task or assignment, and:
- Dividing it up into small steps.
- Keeping within a timescale.
- Putting it in a sensible order.

The planning process is needed if you are to structure your work, and do it in a logical order. It will help you keep to deadlines, and not have to rush at the end. Look at the example Action Plan to help you.

Action Plan:

Task or assignment title:

What are your action steps?   Target dates for completion:

Who will help you?

Part B Communication evidence   Dates completed:
produced:

1.1
1.2

1.3

IT evidence:

Application of Number:

Review and check progress

Regularly check back to your plan to see what you have
achieved and what is left. Are you sticking to time? Are you
working in order? What is going well and what is difficult?
Use the table below to help you.

Review:

First review: Date:

With:

Which action steps have you
completed?

What has gone well?

What has been difficult?

Any changes made to your plan?

What feedback have you been given?

Which action steps remain/new action   Dates:
steps?

What have you achieved?

Part B Communication evidence produced: Dates completed:

1.1

1.2

1.3

IT evidence:

Application of number evidence:

Date of next review:

Your signature: Date:

Assessor signature:

Using your Communication Skills to best advantage:

Performance checklist

Check that you have:

Planned your discussion with one person.

Planned your group discussion.

Planned your reading to make best use of the sources of information.

Made good notes of the main points.

Written and re-written your work until you are satisfied that it is as good as it can be.

Written a memo.
Written an application form.

Written a letter.
Written an essay.

Written a report.

Help desk

Using feedback to improve your work
You should get regular feedback from your teacher/supervisor. This should be specific, with targets for improvement. You should know what you have completed and what you have left to do. Any work not yet finished should be listed with new completion dates.

Portfolio Record sheet Level 1

- Use the sheet below to record your portfolio evidence. This should be evidence from tasks, assignments and problem-solving activities to cover Part B of the unit. The evidence must reach the standard set out in the Communication unit.

- Your teacher/assessor/supervisor must agree with you that your evidence reaches the required standard. Remember, the contexts recorded here should be different from those used above, to practise and develop your skills for Part A.

- You could use the same activity for several components or parts of the unit, or you could use different activities for each part. For example:

→ You could find out about the options available to you in education, post-16 (C1.2), and discuss it with your tutor (C1.1).

→ You could write a summary of your findings for other people to use (C1.3).

→ You could take part in a group discussion about drug abuse (C1.1).

→ You could find out about job opportunities locally (C1.2).

→ You could write a short essay about the way people use their leisure time locally (C1.3).

Remember, do not try to separate the criteria within each component. When you produce some writing, for example, your written evidence must:

Present relevant information in a suitable form
AND
Show that your writing is legible
AND
Show that your spelling, punctuation and grammar is accurate.

Tracking and Recording sheets

Communication Part B	Activity I took part in:	Evidence in my portfolio:	Page Number(s)	Date
1.1 Discussions One-to-one – Straightforward subject				
1.1 Discussions Group – Straightforward subject				
1.2 Reading Information from two documents, including an image Straightforward subject		Image:		
		Document 1:		
		Document 2:		
1.3 Writing Document 1 on a straightforward subject		Image:		
1.2 Writing Document 2 on a straightforward subject with an image.		Image:		

Portfolio-Building at Level 1

The portfolio must show that you have all the skills set out in Part B of the unit. It should show that you can apply your skills in a variety of different situations. Look at the box overleaf for guidance.

- Set up your portfolio at the very beginning.
- Divide the portfolio into: 1) Units
  - 2) Components or parts.
- Listen to the help given to you by your teacher/supervisor.
- Remember it is *quality* not *quantity* which is important.
- Choose examples of evidence which prove your skills and knowledge beyond any doubt.
- Do not be afraid to swap early examples of work for better ones from later in your course.
- It is a good idea to include rough or first drafts of a piece of work, (labelled 'rough drafts') with the final version. This shows that this is your own work, and that you have planned and developed your ideas.
- Put the unit specifications at level 1 in the front.
- Include a contents page at the front, which shows the Key Skills units included, and the order of the work.
- Put an index at the start of each Key Skills unit, showing where each piece of evidence can be found.
- Number all the pages. This is the easiest way for anyone to find individual pieces of evidence. It also means that you can use one piece of evidence to meet the requirements of more than one unit.
- Use portfolio records to list your evidence, and to show which part(s) of the standards it meets.

Level 1 Portfolio example layout:

Contents page

Name:

Organisation:

Key Skills Units and Levels: Include the Communication Level 1 specifications

Section 1: Pages 1–21: Communication Level 1

Section 2: Pages 22–45: Application of Number Level 1

Section 3: Pages 46–63: IT Level 1

Index for Communication Level 1

Page(s)   Communication Portfolio sections

1	Portfolio Record Sheet
2–4	1.1: Discussions: One-to-one
5–11	1.1: Discussions: Group
12–15	1.2: Reading
16–19	1.3: Writing: Document 1
20–21	1.3: Writing: Document 2

Index for IT Level 1

Could also refer to Pages 16–21 of Communication, if these were word processed, and perhaps used as examples of text and images.

Examples of evidence for a Level 1 Communication Portfolio

Page 1: Completed Portfolio Record Sheet

Pages 2–4: 1.1 Discussions: One-to-one

Pages 2–3: Notes of discussion with another student about using your leisure time
Page 4: Observation checklist completed by teacher/supervisor.

Pages 5–11: 1.1 Discussions: Group

Pages 5–8 Notes of discussion in my Foundation GNVQ Health & Social Care group about healthy eating.
Pages 9–10 Questions I asked and answered.
Page 11 Observation checklist completed by my teacher/supervisor.

Pages 12–15: 1.2 Reading

Page 12 The assignment brief with list of chapters, and articles to read from my teacher/supervisor.
Pages 13–14 The notes I made.
Page 15 The list of chapters and sections I used.

Pages 16–19: 1.3 Writing

Document 1 The report from my assignment on a local conservation project.

Pages 20–21: 1.3 Writing

Document 2 The poster I produced to go with my assignment, showing the benefits of the conservation project.

8

Communication Level 2: Developing the Skills and Knowledge in Part A

Introduction

This part of the book will help you to develop and practise your Communication skills as set out in Part A of the unit at level 2. It will also help you get ready for the test at level 2, which is based on Part A.

Remember that at level 2 you need to be able to do everything at level 1, and the extra things at level 2. If you find any of this section difficult, and need more help, look in the level 1 section.

When speaking, listening, reading and writing, it is important to think about:

What you want to say:

What are the important facts, opinions, or points, which you want to make? Are you trying to explain or describe something? Are you giving information?

Why you want to say it:

What is the reason for speaking, reading or writing and what do you intend to achieve? Are you discussing something? Do you want to argue a point of view?

Who you are speaking to or writing to:

How will you know that your style and approach is appropriate? Is it formal enough? What is the setting? Who, and how many people are in your audience?

Ask yourself the questions above, for a variety of everyday situations.

Discussions (Speaking and Listening)

Checklist: When preparing for a discussion:

- Know the topic.
- Know the purpose.
- Know your own role.
- Make notes.
- Try to think of some questions that you could ask others. The questions should be helpful and positive.

Checklist: When taking part in any discussion:

- Make sure that you understand the reason for the discussion.
- The role of those taking part.
- Know who is leading the discussion.
- Speak clearly, using words everyone can understand.
- Make relevant points, give specific examples of what you mean.
- Ask suitable questions. Try to ask an open question, which allows others to respond.
- Show by your body language that you are listening.
- Listen for the tone of people's voices, and the type of language used (vocabulary).
- Watch their gestures.
- Try to understand their point of view.
- Summarise what has been said, to check that everyone has the same understanding.
- Enlarge and develop what has been said, or agreed.

Example:
You are taking part in a discussion with three other people to decide how to collect data on the eating habits of a random sample of 20 people. First of all you need to decide on what the tasks are. Then you must decide who will do what and by when. You need to agree how to work as a team to collect the data. You must decide on how to get a sample of 20 people from your school/college/organisation. What questions will you ask about eating habits? Will you write a questionnaire? How will you use the data? What calculations will you do, and how will you present the data? Even though you are working as a group, you need to keep a record of your individual contributions.

How do you prepare for, and take part in, this discussion?

Go through the checklists:

- Be prepared:
  → Know who you are speaking to, and when.
  → Know how much time you have for the discussion.
  → Take your notes with you.
  → Know which of your points are most important to say for the purpose of the discussion.
- Take part:
  → Listen carefully to what others say.
  → Ask helpful, open questions, which allow others to contribute.
  → Summarise points, check you have understood what has been said.
  → Write notes if you need to.
  → Agree what is to be done, by you and others, and by when.

Example preparation and notes which could be used for the discussion above:

Help desk

Prepare by selecting and reading:
→ Choose the most useful documents to read from the list given.
→ Make a note of your sources and why you chose them.

Make notes of your ideas about:
→ How to get a sample of people: 10 male and 10 female, of the same age.
→ How to collect the data: use a questionnaire, asking them what they eat, how much, at what times.
→ What calculations to do with the data: work out percentages for replies, draw graphs and pie charts of results.
→ What I would like to do: write the questionnaire.
→ Keeping records: I will write an action plan, and write down each thing that I do, and when.

Say these points during the discussion:
→ 'I would like to collect data about the way boys eat compared to girls.'
→ 'I would like to write at least part of the questionnaire.'
→ 'I could work with Mark and George to do this.'
→ 'What do other people think we should ask about eating habits?'
→ 'How could we share the tasks?'
→ 'Do you think the best way to present the data is in bar charts?'
→ 'Who will write down our action plan?'

Help desk

Open Questions

These allow other people to give their own opinion, and are valuable during discussions, because they move things forward. Open questions develop ideas and allow others to join in e.g. 'What do you think about...?', 'Why do you think that happened?'

Closed Questions

Usually need 'Yes' or 'No' answers, or one-word replies e.g. 'What day is it today?' 'Do you want to go to the cinema?'

They are not very helpful in discussions, as they do not encourage people to give their own view or opinion.

In summary. Some Do's and Don'ts.

DO'S ✓

Choose a topic you are interested in and know something about, if you have a choice.
Find out about the topic.
Make notes of the points you want to make.
Speak clearly, using suitable language.
Be able to give information, or present an argument.
Listen to others, and show you are listening.
Make eye contact.
Ask at least one relevant open question. Ask someone to make their point more clearly.
Summarise what has been said as you understand it.

DON'TS X

Be unprepared.
Use slang or jargon.
Be too loud, or too quiet.
Be unsympathetic to what others say.
Ignore others.
Interrupt the person speaking.
Answer without being sure of what the person asked.

Giving a Short Talk

Checklist: When preparing to give a short talk:

- Know and understand the topic.
- Know the purpose.
- Know the audience. How many? Who are they?
- Make notes – this will give the structure of your talk.
- Write a plan which outlines what you intend to say.
- Choose a few pictures, models, or diagrams to make your points.
- Plan time for questions, and think through what you might be asked.
- Practise your talk, by actually saying it out loud.

Checklist: When giving a short talk:

- The talk should last 5–6 minutes, and be given to at least three people.
- Use your notes to help you.
- Try to introduce the topic with an interesting fact, or a story.
- Make sure that your talk has an introduction, a middle and an end.
- Keep looking at your audience, not just at the person in front of you.
- Speak clearly, and loudly enough for people at the back to hear.
- Use gestures to emphasise points.
- Use a picture, chart or model to make a point.
- Demonstrate how to do something.
- Pass something around for people to look at.
- Allow time for questions, or to explain points again.

ACTIVITY

You have been asked to give a short talk to the rest of your group about a hobby/sport or interest, which you enjoy.
You must speak for five minutes, to a group of 15 students.
Use at least one picture, chart or model to help you.

How do you prepare for, and give this short talk?

Go through the checklists:

- Be prepared:
→ Know who you are speaking to, and when.
→ Know how much time you have for the short talk.
→ Take your notes with you.
→ Know which of your points are most important to say, and in what order.

Example notes for use in giving the above talk:

Help desk

Title: <u>A hobby/sport/interest I enjoy</u>
Topic: <u>Formula One Racing</u>

Sources used with reasons:
Encarta – has good general information as a starting point.
The Illustrated History of Formula One – has lots of information from which to choose, especially on races and cars.
Famous Formula One Drivers – has details of the lives of drivers, and all their races.

Topics on which notes were made, with plan and outline of talk:
→ The history of Formula One.
→ The first race (picture).
→ What are Formula One cars?
→ Some famous cars (pictures, models).
→ Some famous drivers (pictures).
→ Some famous races (pictures, diagrams of tracks).
→ Future developments likely in Formula One.
→ Prepare for questions.

Give the talk and take feedback:
→ From teacher/supervisor.
→ From the people in the audience.
→ Self-evaluation.

Help desk

	Four P's for successful talks	
Plan	**Prepare**	**Practise**
	For **Perfect** Performance	
	Remember the more prepared and practised you are the better you will feel, and the better it will go.	

In summary. Some Do's and Don'ts:

DO'S ✓

DON'TS ✗

Be prepared and practised.

Use your plan and follow it.

Present your ideas and points in a sensible order.

Breathe deeply and regularly, to help stay calm if you are nervous.

Wait for the audience to be quiet.

Smile sometimes.

Use gestures for emphasis.

Keep going even if you forget something or miss something out.

Use pictures, plans or diagrams to help.

Be enthusiastic about the topic.

Read from your notes without looking up.

Be afraid to repeat what you say, if people do not understand.

Rush through your talk.

Speak in the same boring tone.

Speak over the audience.

Look frightened.

Move about, fidget, or wave your hands too much.

Don't say 'um' or 'er' too much.

Reading and Summarising:

Checklist: When finding and using different sources:

- Use the library, databases, and the Internet to find your sources of reference from the list given.
- Use the contents page.
- Use the index to look up key words.
- Select the materials you are using, and say why.
- Use a range of sources to give different views and ideas.

DEFINITIONS ▶

Key Skills Words: Extended document means at least three pages long. You must use at least two extended documents as your sources for your portfolio evidence.

Checklist: When skimming, scanning and reading:

- Skim books, articles etc. to get the gist of them.
- Scan materials to pick out the main points and ideas.
- Read the relevant sections in detail.

Checklist: When identifying the type of document and its purpose:

- Recognise the format of the material. Is it a formal letter or memo?
- Recognise the writer's purpose or intention.
- Is s/he presenting an argument? Are opinions given? Is it biased?
- Look for the tone of writing, and types of words used.
- Is it a factual report, or a set of instructions?
- Look for link or signal words like 'therefore', 'whereas' and 'so' to help follow the argument.
- Pick out the main points.

Help desk

When following an argument or line of reasoning:
- There should be a sequence of key points in logical order, which it is possible to follow as the reader.
- Each key point should be explored and developed, and repeated using different words.
- Each key point should be supported with examples and evidence.

Checklist: When summarising information:

- Pick out the key words and meaning.
- Put them into sentences.
- Put your points in a sensible order.
- Number them if it helps.
- Put together a short account, using as few words as possible.

ACTIVITY

You have been asked to write a summary of the career you intend to follow. The instructions given state that you will need to produce the information in a suitable format for the rest of your group, giving them basic information about this career. Look at the example below.

Example:

Help desk

Reading and summarising a career as a Veterinary Nurse

Sources used with reasons:
→ Careers guidance notes from school on working with animals – outlines the types of jobs available.
→ *Veterinary Nursing as a Career* – details entry qualifications, and the type of work involved.
→ *The Veterinary Nurse Record* – gives colleges and courses available, and vets registered as accredited work placements.

The audience: 16 and 17 year olds

Notes made on key points and areas:
→ Qualifications needed.
→ How to get in.
→ Personal skills and experience needed.
→ What the job is like.

→ Salary, holidays.

→ Career opportunities.

The format of the summary:

→ Side of A4 as handout.

Headings to be used in summary:

→ Qualifications required.

→ Age at which you can begin.

→ Relevant experience.

→ Personal qualities.

→ How to apply.

→ A day in the life of.

→ Training.

→ Career developments.

→ Hours, holidays and benefits.

→ Salary.

In summary. Some Do's and Don'ts:

DO'S ✓

Skim, scan, read.
Use contents and index pages.
Identify your main points.
Structure your summary.

DON'TS X

Ignore the writer's purpose.
Make your summary too long.
Make the summary difficult to follow.

Writing

Checklist: When writing:

Make sure that you know the layout for:

A memo:

This is a way of giving information or instructions to one or more people in a formal work situation, or to record what has happened.

● Put the heading 'Memo' or 'Memorandum' in large letters at the top.

- Say who it is to.
- Give the name(s) of anyone else to whom the memo is to be circulated as Copy. Circulated (CC).
- Say who it is from.
- Give the date.
- State the subject of the memo.
- Make the memo short and to the point.

Example:

Help desk

Memo

To: Don, Dave, Mary, Anwen, Nicky
CC: Mr Sudhu
From: Steve
15 Feb 2001

The Enterprise Project

The final presentation of the project will take place on 18 February at 10.00 a.m. in the sixth form common room. Please make sure that you are there at 9.30 a.m. with your notes and handouts. The display board will be available, and we will need to put this together the night before. We will meet on 17 February at 4.30 p.m. to do this. The following items will need to be brought by members of the group, as set out below:

Don: Photographs
Dave: Summary fliers
Mary: Samples of stock
Anwen: Laptop
Nicky: Projector

If anyone has any questions, let me know,
Thank you,

Steve

A business letter:

This is an example of a formal letter.

- Write this type of letter when applying for a job or grant, when writing to any organisation, including Government offices, making a complaint, requesting information or payment.
- Put your name and address in the top right-hand corner.
- Put the name and address of the person you are writing to, underneath, but on the left side of the page.
- Put the date underneath.
- Below the date, start the letter with: 'Dear Sir', 'Dear Madam' or 'Dear Ms Brown'.
- Use formal language, explaining clearly why you are writing.
- End the letter with 'Yours faithfully' if it started 'Dear Sir or Madam' or 'Yours sincerely' if it started with 'Dear Ms Brown'.
- Sign and print your name underneath.

Example:

Help desk

> Steven Chan
> 1 The Pines
> Woodley
> Leafdale
> Cumbria
> LF1 1LF
>
> Mr Roberts
> R&P Marketing
> Molton
> Greater Manchester
> MM1 9TT
>
> 10 January 2001
>
> Dear Mr Roberts,
>
> I am writing on behalf of our cycling club, Leafdale Fliers, following your advertisement in *The Sunday Supplement*. We are very interested in your offer of discount posters and banners for charities. The club is non-profit making, and although not a registered charity, we raise funds for one local and one national charity each year, through our annual sponsored bike ride.
>
> This year we are going to give our proceeds to a local animal rescue centre, and to a national cancer research charity. The bike ride always has a theme, and this year it is a fancy dress ride over 50 miles of hilly

Cumbria. As ever, advertising is our main cost, which makes us very interested in your discount posters and banners for good causes.

We would be very happy to have your company logo on our advertising materials, and we will acknowledge your company in our information to sponsors. In fact if your company would like to sponsor the event itself, by providing funds for the marshals, the post-ride dinner and ball, refreshments, and other equipment, please let me know. Otherwise we would like details of your reduced rate posters and banners, as soon as possible.

I look forward to hearing from you,

Yours sincerely,

Steven Chan

A report:
This could be an account of an event:
- Describe what has happened.
- Explain where it happened.
- Say why it happened.
- State who was part of the event.
- Use a heading and subheadings.
- Make points, use numbers or bullets where sensible.

Example:

(**Help**) **desk**

Super School Sports Day

The Event

The Super School Sports Day on 15 July was well attended by parents and Governors of the school. Every form in the lower school entered the relay competitions, and for the first time, swimming races were held in the newly built pool. The parent combined sack race and the egg and spoon had its biggest entry ever, and certainly raised the loudest cheers of the day.

Presentation

Prizes and cups were presented by the Chair of Governors, Samantha Devas, and local councillor Reginald Straws gave the shields for best House to Hanover, and for individual achievement to Jeremy Redfurn. In the swimming pool Susannah De Faux took the honours.

Sponsors

The school wishes to thank all its sponsors, including Sonic Sports Wear, Acti-pro Food Supplements, and Liquid Life, as major contributors. In addition, school staff and parents, who contributed huge amounts of time and energy to making the event such a success, are to be thanked with afternoon tea, served by the students, on 22 July.

Next Year

Next year, the day is planned to coincide with the school's 25th anniversary celebrations, and promises to be bigger and better than ever. Don't miss the fun!

This is an example of a short report for a school magazine or newsletter, describing an event.

Example:

Help desk

Report on possible transmission routes for Salmonella

The disease

Salmonella is one type of food poisoning, caused by a bacteria also given this name.

The main symptoms are diarrhoea, vomiting and fever, but headaches and stomach pains are also common.

Treatment

Treatment is bed rest, and drinking plenty of fluids, salt and sugar. In severe cases antibiotics can be given.

Transmission

The main routes as shown in the diagram below are through contaminated foods, water, or cooking utensils. Prevention is quite straightforward, involving using hot, soapy water for cleaning hands, surfaces and equipment in the kitchen. Raw and cooked meats should be kept separate. Frozen food must be properly defrosted. Sewage disposal and water treatment must be effective.

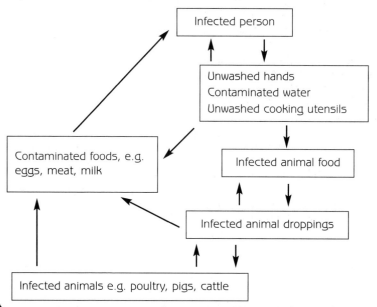

This is an example of a report which includes a flow chart, as an image, to explain more clearly the written points on transmission.

An essay:

This is one way to answer a question, to write an assignment, or perhaps a piece of coursework.

- The most important thing is to answer the question.
- Plan your essay, so that it has a beginning, a middle, and an end.
- Write a rough draft after your plan.
- The rough draft has key points, key words, your basic ideas, the order of your essay.
- Write clearly, in sentences.
- Use paragraphs to divide the essay into sections; beginning, middle and end.

Example:

Help desk

Essay title: The Life and Works of Charles Darwin

Charles Darwin was born in Shrewsbury, on 12 February 1809. His father Robert Darwin was a doctor, who wanted his son to follow in his footsteps. His mother was from the family of the famous potter Josiah Wedgwood. She died when Charles was only eight years old.

He went to Shrewsbury School as a boarder, but often came home for visits. He did not do well at school, and disappointed his father. He showed no interest in medicine. His father sent him to Edinburgh University to study medicine anyway, but he did not do well. Darwin fainted at the sight of blood, which made it very unlikely that he would be a surgeon, as his father wanted.

He was always a great collector, starting as a boy he collected insects and shells. Later when it became obvious, even to his father, that he would never make a doctor, he was sent to Christ's College Cambridge. He studied to enter the Church. As he had no great ambition, he seemed content to end up as a country vicar. He wasted his time at Cambridge, just about passing his degree, and spending a lot of time singing, drinking and playing cards. The only useful things he did were to continue collecting beetles, and to learn to shoot.

In August 1831, two Cambridge professors who he knew, wrote to Darwin inviting him to join HMS Beagle as official naturalist, during a voyage to explore South America. These invitations eventually led to Darwin's theories on evolution being written, and they altered the course of his life dramatically. At first Darwin turned down the invitations, because his father did not want him to go. His father was persuaded by his brother-in-law, Josiah Wedgwood, to let his son join the ship.

Darwin spent many months waiting for the ship to be ready to sail. During this time he was ill with rashes and chest pains, which were probably due to stress. He met the man commanding the ship, Captain Fitzroy, in September and liked him from the start. He finally set sail from Plymouth, on the Beagle, on 27 December 1831. He discovered on the voyage that he was no sailor, becoming seasick many times.

When Darwin reached the tropics, three months later, and landed at Bahia in Brazil, he was totally thrilled and absorbed by the jungle. It was full of life, plants and animals that he had never dreamed of. He also noticed straight away how dangerous the jungle was, with animals fighting to survive all the time. He collected thousands of specimens on the coast, and on his journeys inland. He was a very enthusiastic collector, a fit and healthy young man (see overleaf), enjoying himself greatly. He started to collect fossils, found South of Buenos Aires. Darwin realised that these bones were very old, and belonged to animals no longer seen. He started to wonder about the idea of the whole world being created at the same time. He began to doubt that the earth, and all the living things on it, had been formed at one time.

In Tierra del Fuego (see map) Darwin and the crew had a very bad time. The weather was terrible, and the land bleak and cold. Darwin and Fitzroy led an expedition to explore and try to start a colony. They were almost killed when a glacier fell into the sea, and they nearly lost their boat. It was Darwin who saved them, and Fitzroy was so grateful that he named a mountain 'Mount Darwin' in his honour. When they returned to the camp, they found that native people had taken all the food and goods which the crew had.

They sailed soon after this, to the Falkland Islands. Fitzroy seemed badly affected by what had happened in Tierra del Fuego, and became difficult to talk to. Darwin became more confident, and was very much

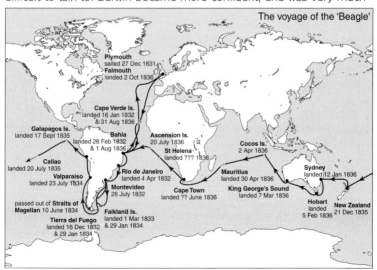

The voyage of the 'Beagle'

Plymouth
sailed 27 Dec 1831
Falmouth
landed 2 Oct 1836

Cape Verde Is.
landed 16 Jan 1832
& 31 Aug 1836

Galapagos Is.
landed 17 Sept 1835

Bahia
landed 28 Feb 1832
& 1 Aug 1836

Ascension Is.
20 July 1836

St Helena
landed ??? 1836

Cocos Is.
2 Apr 1836

Callao
landed 20 July 1835

Valparaiso
landed 23 July 1834

Rio de Janeiro
landed 4 Apr 1832

Montevideo
26 July 1832

Mauritius
landed 30 Apr 1836

Cape Town
landed ?? June 1836

King George's Sound
landed 7 Mar 1836

Sydney
landed 12 Jan 1836

passed out of Straits of
Magellan 10 June 1834

Falkland Is.
landed 1 Mar 1833
& 29 Jan 1834

Tierra del Fuego
landed 16 Dec 1832
& 29 Jan 1834

Hobart
landed
5 Feb 1836

New Zealand
21 Dec 1835

enjoying his life as a naturalist. He had a great deal of energy. He lived on raw meat and ostrich eggs for much of the time, and was completely at home in this wild land.

Darwin travelled around the edge of South America into the Pacific Ocean, as the map below shows. The voyage around Cape Horn was rough, as it was winter and bitterly cold. Some of the crew died because of the conditions. He explored the Andes, and discovered fossilised shells high in the mountains. He realised that this land had once been in the sea. He began to put together his ideas on the history of South America. When he got back to the Beagle, Fitzroy was mentally ill, and suicidal. Darwin was calm, and persuaded him to carry on with the voyage.

He landed in the Galapagos Islands in 1835, and was fascinated by the different plants and animals on each small island. He noticed the finches and their different beaks, and the Giant Tortoises. He was also fascinated by the lizards which lived in the sea, and the strange birds, some with blue, and some with pink feet. He made many notes and observations in his journal. He travelled back via New Zealand, Australia and the Indian Ocean. In the Cocos Islands, he noticed again the different animals not seen anywhere else.

When he got home, after five years away, he spent two years organising his collection of fossils, plants and animals. He wrote up his diary of the voyage of the Beagle, and was surprised when it was a bestseller. Then he married his cousin, Emma Wedgwood, and had children. He was an active, fit and healthy man at this time, as his picture shows.

He moved to Downe in Kent to carry on writing, but he was ill for a lot of the time, seeming to be troubled by his work and his ideas about evolution. He was only able to work in the mornings, and spent the rest of the day reading, walking and resting. His wife looked after him when he was ill.

He published the *Origin of Species* in 1859, explaining in it his ideas about evolution. He had to write it quickly, to beat Alfred Wallace, who had a theory like Darwin's. This also sold out on the first day, and caused an outcry. Darwin never got involved in the discussions and debates which followed. He published *The Descent of Man* in 1871, and as his ideas were generally accepted by then, this caused little fuss. He had the support of some famous and respected scientists, who helped to get his ideas and theories accepted.

After this, Darwin led a quiet life in Kent. He wrote other books about plants, orchids and worms. One of his sons, Horace, helped him with his work on worms, by building a 'wormstone' to see how fast worms could break down the soil. He was very famous by now, but he stayed out of public life. He was never in good health in later life, but he was very happy at home with his family. He also had a lot of money by then.

He became very ill in 1882, with sickness and fainting fits. He died in his sleep on 19 April 1882. His wife and children wanted to bury him at home in Downe, but he was so famous by then that he was buried in Westminster Abbey.

Help desk

Straightforward subject means an everyday or ordinary topic, which you are learning about in a course of study, or which you come across in the workplace. In the essay above the subject is straightforward, because it is about the aspects of Darwin's life which are easy to understand. The ideas are straightforward: there is information about his life and family, and about his journey. His theories are mentioned by name but not explained or explored.

If the essay was about the complex and technical aspects of his work, or if it covered sensitive issues in his life, or explored the effects and sense of outrage his theories caused, then the topic would be dealt with in a complex way. This would mean that the essay could be used at level 3. To do so, the other criteria for writing would need to be met e.g. writing complex sentences, and using technical language. Spelling, punctuation and grammar would also need to be used at level 3.

Help desk

Images must be used to make a point, or explain something. They must be a part of the document as a whole, and make it easier to understand. If the document would make less sense without the images, then they are being used correctly.

In the example report on Salmonella, the chart explains how the disease is spread, and shows more information than in the writing alone. It explains more routes for transmission.

In the essay on Charles Darwin, the picture of him is referred to in the text as showing him as a fit, healthy man. The map of the voyage of the Beagle, shows where and when he sailed, and links to passages about landing in South America, making trips inland, and going to the Galapagos Islands.

Help desk

Extended document means at least three pages long. One of your pieces of writing will need to be an extended document at level 2. This means about three pages of text. It is likely to be a report, an essay, coursework or an assignment. This extended document must be the one which contains an image. In the examples in this chapter, the only three-page document is the essay. Since it has an image, it could be used as evidence of an extended document.

There is no need to over-do the length of your Communication written evidence, though. Remember that your work will be assessed for accuracy of spelling, grammar and punctuation. Although a few errors would be allowed in a long document, it is easier to maintain accuracy in a three-page document, than a 30-page one.

An application form:

Help desk

Savalot Supermarket
Application form

Complete this form in block capitals
Last name:
First names:
Address:

Telephone number:
Date of birth:

Names and addresses of schools/colleges attended since age 11:
Dates:
From:
To:

Examinations taken or about to be taken:
GCSE:
Grade:
Date:

AS/A:
Grade:
Date:

GNVQ:

Level:

Grade:

Date:

List any other courses and qualifications taken or about to be taken.

Give details of any work experience or part-time work you have had.

Interests and activities including voluntary work, clubs, hobbies and sport. This could include activities inside or outside school.

Give details of any special achievements or positions of responsibility, such as prefect, Duke of Edinburgh Award.

Please say why you are interested in this post, and why you consider yourself suitable.

Signature:

Date:

Structure and organise your work to make it easy to follow, using a suitable style:

- Choose the most appropriate form and style.
- Use paragraphs.
- Indent the first line, or leave a line between paragraphs.
- Headings should be used to divide into main areas.
- Sub-headings for further divisions.
- Use these divisions to make the text easy on the eye.
- Use a suitable style, such as a technical report, a set of instructions, descriptive writing, a personal letter expressing your feelings, to suit the purpose of your writing.
- Keep to the same tense.

Help desk

Paragraphs are groups of sentences about the same subject or idea.

Show new paragraphs by indenting the first line, or leave a line between paragraphs.

Proofread your work and re-draft, to make sure that you have:

Spelt everyday words correctly by:
- Identifying and circling new words.
- Checking the spelling is correct.
- Keeping a spelling book, with a list of words.
- Adding new words to your list.
- Practising your spelling every day.
- Covering the word, trying to spell it, check your spelling.
- Adding unusual or technical words to your list.
- Using a dictionary.

Help desk

Examples of words you should be able to spell, but which are easily misspelled:

there	their	they're	thieve
belief	believe 17	receive 1	achieve 14
choose	chose	choice 19	cheque
which	witch	whole	where
height	weight 20	weird	were
leisure 6	pleasure	acquire 10	accurate 15
seize 5	size	says	science 12
weather	whether	Wednesday 8	wear
humour	honour 7	humorous 9	holiday
appalling 11	anxious 3	accommodate 2	accelerate 18
yacht 4	yield 16	vicious 13	vegetable

Checklist: Using a dictionary:
- Words are listed in dictionaries in alphabetical order.
- The word is shown in bold.
- Then there is a letter, which tells you what type of word it is.
- Then there are explanations of the word's meaning(s).
- There are also abbreviations, and examples of use of the word, followed by the origin of the word.

Help desk

friend

Type of word = n = noun
Meanings = 1. a person well
known to another and regarded
with liking, affection, and loyalty;
an intimate. 2. an acquaintance or
associate. 3. an ally in a fight or
cause; supporter....
Uses = 6. be friends (with). 7.
make friends (with)
Origin = Old English *freond*...

Checklist: Using a spell-checker:

- The spell-checker does not check meaning.
- It cannot tell you if 'their' should be spelt 'there' in your sentence.
- If you tell it how to spell an unusual word, make sure the word is correct, otherwise the computer will always tell you to spell it wrongly.

Follow the rules of grammar, to put words into the correct order in complex sentences, to make sure:

- The verb agrees with the subject.
- The tense is used consistently.
- The sentence is divided up using commas.
- You can use link words such as 'but', 'then' and 'because'.

Examples:

She was very pleased with the gift, but would have liked to open it later.
We were keen to get to the game on time, because we had to buy our tickets.

Use correct punctuation:

- Punctuation is used to put a pause or space between words.
- This helps to make more sense of the words, and to give emphasis, when speaking or reading.
- You should be able to use commas, apostrophes and inverted commas.
- Commas show a short pause, within a sentence, to divide it into different parts. They can alter the meaning of the sentence, or

separate the items in a list. The pause shown by a comma is shorter than that shown by a full stop.

- Apostrophes show 'belonging to', or the place where letters are missing.

Help desk

Remember it's = it is, with the apostrophe for the missing 'i'. 'Its' has no apostrophe because it is like his or hers, when something belongs to it.

- Inverted commas or quotation marks show someone is speaking. They also show quotations from books, which someone else wrote, the titles of songs and poems, or slang or technical words. The inverted commas come at the beginning and the end of the quote '   ' with a comma in front, if in the middle of a sentence.

Examples:

Jane's Jaguar is very fast, but James' tractor goes anywhere.

The dog has had its day, but the cat is waiting for hers.

He didn't want to stop and say goodbye, because his train was leaving.

He's the one with all the money.

'Don't do that,' she said, 'because you may fall into the water.'

Help desk

Type of word:	How it is used:
Verb	A verb is used to describe an action.
	Examples: to run, to play, to hide, to laugh, to fight, to talk, to write.
	Verbs change depending on the tense, which tells you if the action happened in the past, is happening now, or will happen in the future.
	The form of the verb must agree with the subject.
	Examples: She did play with the dog. We fed the cat.
Noun	A noun is the name of a person, a place, an animal, plant or a thing.
	Examples: Peter, Peterborough, panther, primrose, pencil.
	The names of people, places, organisations, days, months and seasons are given capital letters
Adjective	An adjective describes a noun or a pronoun.
	Examples: large, small, bad, yellow.
Adverb	An adverb describes a verb, or an adjective.
	Examples: quickly, sadly, good, badly.
Pronoun	A pronoun is used instead of a noun.
	Examples: she, he, it.

Help desk

Tense: The tense tells you if the action happened in the past, is happening now, or will happen in the future. These are the past, present and future tenses.

In summary. Some Do's and Don'ts.

DO'S ✓

Use a suitable style of writing.

Follow the rules for different types of writing.

Plan and structure reports and essays.

Use pictures, charts and diagrams to make your points more clearly.

Proofread and re-draft.

DON'TS X

Wander away from the point or the question.

Spell words wrongly.

Use wrong punctuation.

Ignore the rules of grammar.

Communication Level 2: Practice Test Questions on Part A

Introduction

Now that you have developed and practised the Communication Skills set out in Part A of the unit, you are ready to try some short answer and multiple choice questions. If you find any of the questions difficult go back to Chapter 9 for more help before moving on with the book.

Here are some short answer questions to check that you have all the skills and knowledge as set out in Part A. These are followed by example multiple-choice questions, showing the type of questions in the external tests. The external questions will not have questions on discussions or giving talks.

Short answer questions

Discussions (Speaking and Listening)

ACTIVITY

Prepare for and take part in a discussion with at least three people about the advertising of chocolate and sweets on television and in the press. You should make notes and be prepared to ask and answer questions.

1. You could decide to find out about particular types of products, or you could consider the different types of advertisements you have seen. Try to find out about different aspects so that each person has a different area to contribute to the discussion.

2. Take part in the discussion. Try to contribute as much as you can. Use your notes. Do not interrupt others. Be positive and helpful in your contributions. Summarise and develop your points.

3. Now fill in the self evaluation about the discussion below. Try to be as honest as possible. Use your evaluation to improve on future discussions, such as those suggested in parts 2 and 3.

Self Evaluation:

When I spoke I made the following points:

I listened to these people speak:

I answered these questions:

Did you interrupt anyone? Yes ☐   No ☐

I asked these questions:

Something I liked about the discussion:

Something which I would change in my next discussion is:

Ask one of the other people in the discussion or an observer to complete the audience evaluation to support your own views above:

Audience Evaluation:

Something which I liked about the way .... took part in the discussion is:

Something which .... did very well in the discussion is:

Something which .... could have done better in the discussion is:

Short Talk

ACTIVITY

Make notes for a short talk about planning and going on a holiday, or a residential trip with your organisation:

1. Plan your talk, make notes, which are in a sensible order. Find an image to make one of your points: this

could be a picture, a sketch plan or a model. In this case it could be a map of your journey; photographs of activities on the trip; something which explains a part of the culture of a foreign country; or an item of equipment used on an expedition.

2. Give the talk, lasting 5–6 minutes, to at least three people.

3. Now fill in the self evaluation about the talk below. Try to be as honest as possible. Use it to improve on future talks which you give, such as those suggested in parts two and three of this book.

Self-Evaluation:

When I spoke I made the following points:

I answered these questions:

Something I liked about the talk:

Something which I would change in my next short talk is:

The structure of the talk was/was not easy for people to follow.

I used an image to explain ....

Ask one of the other people in the audience to complete the audience evaluation below to support your own views above:

Audience evaluation

Something which I liked about the way .... gave the talk is:

Something which .... did very well in the talk is:

Something which .... could have done better during the talk is:

Reading and Summarising

ACTIVITY

Summarise the article below on the dangers of hands-free mobile phone kits. Say what the dangers are, and what the evidence is based on. What is the intention of the writer in presenting the information in this way?

MOBILE phone hands-free kits ARE dangerous, new research shows.

The most recent study backs claims that they TREBLE the amount of microwave radiation emitted around the head.

The Consumers Association report, due to be published later this year, will directly contradict Government research which claimed the kits cut radiation emissions by 80 per cent.

Association chiefs had hoped their new research would clear up the confusion over the safety of the hands-free kits.

But they now fear it is likely to put them at loggerheads with the Government.

An insider said last night: 'This is likely to be another case of each camp refusing to believe the other. We believe there are problems with the Government research into hands-free sets. We have conducted an investigation into their methods – and we think there are difficulties.

'We have also re-done our own research into radiation levels to make sure there is no mistake.

'The debate is a long way from over.'

An earlier Consumers Association report was criticised by the Department of Trade and Industry for not measuring exactly how much radiation from hands-free kits entered the brain.

The measurement is known as Specific Absorption Rate (SAR).

The DTI then did its own research – which included SARs – to come up with the 80 per cent reduction figure.

But Association scientists now insist the DTI's results are not reliable.

Mobile phones have already been linked to cancer, memory loss, multiple sclerosis and headaches.

In May, a report urged parents to limit children's time on mobiles – and said phone masts should not be built near schools and old people's homes.

Three weeks ago, the *Sunday Mirror* revealed the Government had done a U-turn on its policy on masts – despite endorsing the inquiry recommending caution on the siting of the masts.

More than 31 million people use mobile phones in Britain.

Turn to page 117 for one possible summary.

ACTIVITY

You have a Saturday job in a travel agent, and are answering enquiries for a customer. Using the information given below from a holiday brochure, identify the following holidays available for two people sharing a twin room. You will need to obtain information from the text, and numbers given in the table, to answer these questions.

Hotel du Théatre TT

A small family-run hotel, ideally situated in the central pedestrianised area of the city, this comfortable hotel boasts 18th Century architecture but modern-style decoration and service.
LOCATION – Close to the Grand Théatre and the Place de la Comedie, a short stroll to the River Garonne.
FACILITIES – The hotel has a small lounge and bar in the reception area for guests only, bedrooms are bright and comfortable with telephone, and full central heating for winter visitors.
Rooms: 24
Map Ref: 1

Bayonne Etche-Ona TT

The 18th Century Bayonne Etche-Ona makes an ideal base for exploring the city and surrounding vineyards. Renovated rooms are furnished with antiques.
LOCATION – Near the Church Notre Dame and the cloisters of the Dominican Convent, in the Gold Triangle of Bordeaux, close to all the main shops.
FACILITIES – Lounge, bar area. Rooms are air-conditioned with minibar, satellite TV, hairdryer, telephone and trouser press.
Rooms: 65
Map Ref: 2

Sainte Catherine TT

This charming and luxurious hotel combines elegance with friendliness, thus creating a great welcome to the city.
LOCATION – In the heart of the city with plenty of bars, restaurants and shops nearby.
FACILITIES – Lounge, bar. Rooms are bright and spacious with air-conditioning, telephone, satellite TV, radio, safety-deposit box and minibar.
Rooms: 84
Map Ref: 3

YOUR HOLIDAY PRICE

Prices in £s per person sharing a twin room with breakfast

Destination code: BOD

No. of Nights	2	3	4	5	Extra night pppn
HOTEL DU THÉATRE					
18 Nov–20 Dec	225	243	270	293	17
1 Jan–30 Jun	246	262	283	302	21
1 Jul–31 Aug	289	308	326	345	21
1 Sep–31 Dec	246	264	283	302	21
BAYONNE ETCHE-ONA					
18 Nov–20 Dec	255	280	314	349	30
1 Jan–30 Apr	268	299	338	368	36
1 May–30 Jun	283	312	344	381	36
1 Jul–31 Aug	315	348	377	407	33
1 Sep–31 Oct	277	311	344	375	36
1 Nov–31 Dec	273	304	343	373	36
SAINTE CATHERINE					
18 Nov–20 Dec	265	294	333	372	35
1 Jan–31 March	278	313	348	383	36
1 Apr–30 Jun	291	333	372	411	42
1 Jul–31 Aug	335	373	415	449	42
1 Sep–31 Oct	294	333	372	411	42
1 Nov–26 Dec	278	313	348	383	37
27 Dec–31 Dec	300	340	375	375	42

PRICE INCLUDES: Return flights – Accommodation – Breakfast – Taxes, including Passenger Service Charge – Guidebook
Departure dates on or between dates given.

YOUR TRAVEL OPTIONS

BRITISH AIRWAYS
AIR FRANCE

TRANSPORT DETAILS

From	Carrier	Frequency Dep UK/ Arr UK	Supplement Mon–Thurs	Fri–Sun
Gatwick	**British Airways**	**Daily**		
18 Nov 99–31 Dec 00			0	0
Heathrow	**Air France**	**Daily**		
18 Nov–31 Dec 99		via Paris	0	0
1 Jan–31 Dec			–18	–18
Birmingham	**Air France**	**Daily**		
18 Nov–24 Dec 99		via Paris	65	65
25 Dec–31 Dec 99			24	24
1 Jan–30 Jun, 1 Sep–31 Dec			–5	–5
1 Jul–31 Aug			0	0
Humberside/ Teesside	**Air France**	**Daily**		
1 Jan–30 Jun, 1 Sep–31 Dec			–5	–5
1 Jul–31 Aug			0	0
Newcastle/ Edinburgh/ Glasgow	**Air France**	**Daily**		
18 Nov–24 Dec 99		via Paris	103	103
25 Dec–31 Dec 99			64	64
1 Jan–31 Dec			–5	–5

a) Which holiday costs less than £450 per person for six nights, between 25 and 31 Dec, departing from Birmingham, on a Saturday, including all the supplements.

b) Which hotel would be best for visiting the vineyards of Bordeaux? Say why.

c) How much would a four-night stay cost in August at the Sainte Catherine per person, departing from Gatwick?

d) Which hotel would you recommend to a customer who said that they wanted to be close to the city centre, in a small hotel, with its own lounge, and central heating?

Turn to page 118 for the answers.

ACTIVITY

Write a title for each of the following six images labelled A–F.

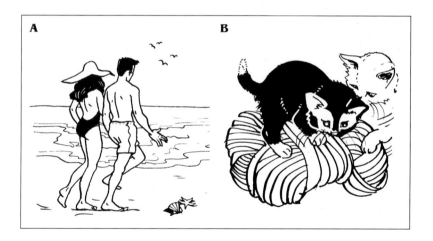

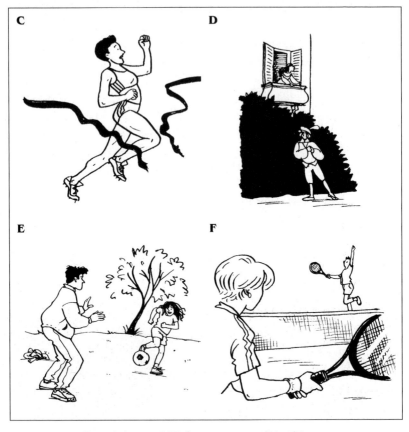

Turn to page 118 for some possible titles.

Writing

ACTIVITY

Improve the spelling, grammar and punctuation in the following letter:

Dear Sir,

Me and my mates was passing you're shop the other day and sore that u wanted some help on a saturday I fink Id be realy good working in youre shop. I no a lot about sport cloths and realy like them to becos I where them all the time If u want me to sea u for an intervu I cold come on wensday after skool I hop u will gimme a job

Thanks – see you.

Chris

O I forgot to ask whats the pay like

Turn to page 118 for an improved version.

ACTIVITY

Write a description of the scene shown in this photograph, of St. Paul's Cathedral, after the worst night of the Blitz, on 10 May 1941:

Turn to page 119 for an example description.

Short answer questions on page 113–117

Reading

Summary of the dangers of hands-free mobile phones:

The Consumers Association is to publish a report later this year, based on research, which shows that hands-free sets actually treble the amount of radiation emitted. Government research into this safety issue shows that the kits reduce emissions by 80%. Earlier reports were criticised for not actually measuring the radiation, as Specific Absorption Rate (SAR). Since over 31 million people use mobile phones, the levels of emissions, linked with health risks, such as cancer, memory loss, headaches, and multiple sclerosis, are very important.

Travel brochure answers:
a) Hotel du Théâtre or Bayonne Etche-Ona.
b) Bayonne Etche-Ona, because it is nearest the vineyards.
c) £415
d) Hotel du Théâtre.

Images: some possible titles:
A True romance
B Pets Playtime
C Victory!
D Love's path is never easy
E A family team
F Mixed doubles

Writing

Improved letter:

> Simon Smith
> 3 Bear Close
> Goldy Wood
> Epsom
> Surrey
> GG6 3BB
> Tel: 01990 654321

Mr Khan
Slinky Sports
The High Street
Golford
Surrey
GG0 ILF
15 November 2000

Dear Sir,

I was passing your shop recently, and I saw that you want more staff on Saturdays. I would really like to work in your shop, because I am very interested in sport and sports clothes. I wear sports clothes myself, and would enjoy helping your customers to choose clothes from your shop.

If you would like to speak to me, or to interview me for this Saturday job, the best day for me would be Wednesday, after school, from 4.30 p.m. or on a Saturday. Please contact me to arrange a time, as I would very much like to work in your shop.

Yours sincerely

Simon Smith

Description of the scene of St. Paul's:

St. Paul's Cathedral stands majestic and untouched by last night's blitz of London, the worst bombing yet seen of this war. The great dome towers above a scene of total devastation, with many of the buildings reduced to rubble. Those left standing are scarred and burnt, from the incendiary bombs dropped for hour after hour, throughout the night.

Multiple-choice questions

Now try these multiple-choice questions, which will test your Communication skills in the same way as the one-hour external assessment. Dictionaries are not allowed in the test. You will have 60 minutes to answer 40 questions in the text.

In each case the question is followed by four possible answers. Only one of these is the right answer. Choose the word, sentence, or phrase, which you think is correct, and write down the letter which matches it. This is your answer.

Example:
The waiter was asked to return all the wine glasses to .... correct place on the shelf.

Choose the correct word to fill the gap above

A   there
B   they're
C   their
D   th'ere

If you think the answer is 'their' put the letter C. (This is the correct answer.)

The answers to the following 12 example questions can be found on page 125. Try to answer the questions yourself, before you check them. Remember that dictionaries are not allowed in the test. You will have to answer 40 questions in one hour.

1. In which sentence would you use inverted commas?

A He was thought to have been very upset by the scandal.
B I am very upset by this scandal, he said.
C He would have been very upset by the scandal.
D I wondered if the scandal would be upsetting for him.

2. Read the sentence below, and pay close attention to the spelling and punctuation.

"The dog should have had it's dinner now," said the farmer, "She has been waiting long enough."

There is an error in this sentence. What is it?

A Inverted commas are wrongly used
B The word <u>she</u> should have a small letter
C The commas are in the wrong place
D The apostrophe is used wrongly

Questions 3–5 are based on the diagrams below, taken from a safety leaflet for wiring electric plugs. They are not in the order in which they appear in the leaflet. Each diagram has a heading and a set of instructions.

3. Which of the diagram instructions contains a spelling mistake?

A Diagram 1
B Diagram 2
C Diagram 3
D Diagram 4

4. Match the heading with diagram 1

1   Undo brass screw on lower side of plug

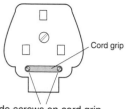

Cord grip

Undo screws on cord grip, to allow cord to pass through (do not remove)

2   Tighten screw up to hold both sides of plug together

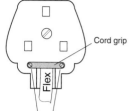

Cord grip

Flex

Tighten screws on cord, so that it is held firmly in place

3   Earth = Green and Yellow or Green wire

32mm
22mm

Fuse
12mm
Cord grip
Live = Brown or Red

Neutral = Blue or Black wire

Cut the wires to lengths shown. Remove plastic sleeve for finel 6mm of each wire insert cord into grip

4   Undo screws to allow wires into (do not remove) terminals. Twist exposed ends of wires together, or solder together. Push into brass terminals. Screw down firmly, holding wires in place

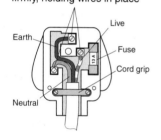

Earth
Live
Fuse
Cord grip
Neutral

A   Preparing the wires
B   Connecting the wires
C   Opening the plug
D   Putting the plug together

5. Put the diagrams into a sensible order.

A   1, 3, 4, 2
B   2, 3, 4, 1
C   1, 2, 4, 3
D   1, 4, 3, 2

Questions 6 and 7 are based on the chart of nutritional information for some well-known foods. Study the chart below for your answers.

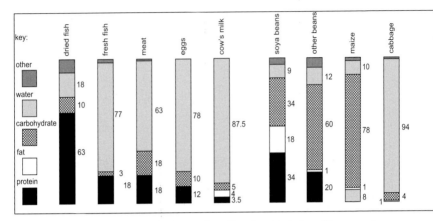

6. Which of the following foods contains the most protein?

A soya beans
B meat
C fresh fish
D other beans

7. In the chart, which of these foods contain the least carbohydrate?

A eggs
B cow's milk
C meat
D dried fish

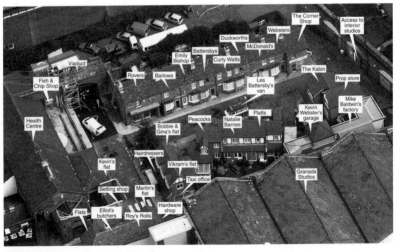

Photograph by Chris Neill.

8. The photograph of the Coronation Street set above shows that

A   The Barlows live in the same street as Martin.
B   The Duckworths live opposite the hairdressers.
C   The Duckworths live next door but one to the McDonalds.
D   The Barlows live next door but one to the Battersbys.

Questions 9–10 are based on the article below.

CAMELOT chiefs stand to pick up an £8 million bonus from the chaos over who will run the National Lottery in the future.

The company, which is bidding for a second seven-year contract, is expected to be asked by the Government to continue temporarily while legal wrangles are settled.

Ministers are this week expected to approve an emergency two-month contract to keep the game ticking over. And that means an extra £8 million on top of an expected £48.5million this year.

The battle between Camelot and Sir Richard Branson's People's Lottery is set to delay the award of a new licence from next September. And, to prevent the game from collapse, Camelot is to be asked to fill the gap pending a final decision.

The National Lottery Commission hopes to choose a winner by the end of November.

But that leaves only 10 months to set up a new operation. Both bidders have said they need at least 12 months.

A spokeman for the Commission said costs would absorb much of the extra bonus.

9. Temporarily in line 4 of the second paragraph means.

A   for a long time
B   for ever
C   permanently
D   for a short time

10. A new licence in line 4 of paragraph four means

A   permission
B   freedom
C   control
D   prevention

Questions 11–12 are based on the article from *The Sun* newspaper below.

A BRAVE builder was stabbed to death as he chased a burglar he disturbed at his house.

John Pettit, who was 60, clambered over fences to pursue the thief through three neighbouring gardens.

But then the raider stopped, pulled out a knife or a screwdriver and plunged it into him. John – a gentle, family man – died minutes later.

He was murdered soon after he and wife Brenda returned following an evening out and found an intruder in their home.

The killing shocked people living hear the £350, 000 semi in Pinner, north-west London.

Jack and Clare Craigie-Williams knew John for 30 years.

Jack, 74, said: "He was strong and wouldn't have stood for anybody breaking in."

"He was the kind of guy who would have a go."

"He was very house proud and he had done a lot of alterations on it himself."

And Sandra Schneider, 48, said: "It does not surprise me that he did something like that."

"People will always try to protect their property."

Solicitor Tony Partree, another neighbour, said: "John was quite a stocky fellow but not aggressive. You could tell he was a real family man. His wife must be devastated." Louise Selman, 24, who lived next door to the couple for 15 years said: "I'm not surprised he went for the burglar."

"I think anyone would if they found someone in their house."

A woman living three doors from John's house found him dying and covered with blood in her back garden soon after the stabbing on Thursday night.

Escaped

She dialled 999 and cops poured into the area.

A helicopter with thermal imaging equipment joined the hunt for the killer but he escaped. A police spokeswoman said: "The couple found a door open when they got home. The man went to investigate. His wife heard him shout, then the sound of an altercation. She heard him leave the house and she called police."

Officers found a "number of small items" from John's home in the garden.

But they were still searching for the murder weapon.

One detective said: "We don't know exactly what it was."

"It could have been a knife, or a screwdriver."

John's blue Mercedes van was outside and a blue metallic Mercedes car was in the garage.

Ten other houses nearby were sealed off in the investigation.

John's grieving wife was being cared for by relatives. She has two adult sons.

---

11. Which sentence best describes the *Sun's* point of view?

A It is wrong to try to defend your property, if you are burgled.

B The Government should protect the victims of burglary who try to defend their property.

C The Government should increase the penalties against anyone who shoots a burglar in defence of their home.

D It is right to stop people from defending their own homes from burglars.

12. The *Sunday Mirror* is an example of which type of newspaper?

A broadsheet

B magazine

C tabloid

D large

The answers to questions 1–12 on pages 119–125:

 1. B
 2. D
 3. C
 4. C
 5. A
 6. A
 7. B
 8. D
 9. D
10. A
11. B
12. C

If you got some answers wrong, you may need to practise:

- Questions 1–3 Spelling, grammar and punctuation.
- Questions 4–8 Using and understanding images.
- Questions 9–11 Understanding the meaning of words and sentences.
- Question 12 Formats of documents.

Communication Level 2: Activities for Practice (Part A) or Assessment (Part B)

Introduction

This part of the book will help you to practise all the skills and check that you have all the knowledge set out in Part A of the Communication unit, and that you are ready to use these skills in assignments, tasks and everyday situations in work, school or college, to produce evidence for your portfolio.

In this section you will also start to get ideas for assignments, which you can use as evidence in your portfolio. This is needed to meet part B of the unit.

When you have practised your skills, you will be ready to plan activities and assignments, to apply your skills, and to show what you can do in your portfolio of evidence. Whether you use the activities and tasks here, to continue to develop and pratise your skills, OR you use them in your portfolio for assessment is up to you. There are record sheets in this chapter for Part A if you are still practising your skills. There are also tracking and recording sheets here, for use in your portfolio if you are ready to be assessed on your evidence.

Use the following sheet to keep an on-going record of your developing skills and knowledge. Use it to record examples of tasks and assignments, which have helped you to practise your skills. You may only need one example here, or you may need more than two, depending upon your skill level when you start this unit.

Communication Part A	One example of an activity which has helped me develop and practise my skills is:	One example of an activity which has helped me develop and practise my skills is:
2.1a Discussions Research information. Make notes. Make useful points. Listen carefully for tone, and watch gestures. Use your own body language to show you are listening. Ask questions.		
2.1b Short talk Research topic. Make notes. Speak clearly. Use standard English. Structure the talk, to put points in a sensible order. Use image(s) to make points.		
2.2 Reading and Summarising Use different sources. including extended documents (3 pages) Skim sources picking out main points. Scan texts. Identify arguments and opinions. Summarise for a talk, essay or report.		
2.3 Writing Write: Letter Memo Notes Report Essay Application form Use images Structure work with: Paragraphs Headings Sub-headings Choose suitable style e.g. formal or informal Proofread, and redraft Use accurate: Spelling Grammar Punctuation Use dictionary/spell-checker		

2.1 Discussions and Short Talk

You could use any example of a discussion and a short talk, but if you want to use the evidence in your portfolio, someone needs to observe you and record your skills as having met the criteria as shown below. You will need to be supervised for this to take place and for your assessor to confirm your skills. You could use a video or audio tape as part of your evidence. You can help this process by keeping your own records and reflections of the discussion using the tracking and recording sheets like those which follow on pages 131–132. These sheets can be used to show how your skills are developing. They could also be part of your portfolio evidence, to help show that you can use your skills in different situations.

Examples of discussions you could take part in to practise and apply your skills:

- Comparing the costs of renting and buying a house or flat (Group).
- Getting help if worried about being pregnant/having a partner who is pregnant (Group).
- Careers interview with a careers advisor (One-to-one).
- A job interview(One-to-one).
- Discussion with a client (One-to-one) who wants to:
  A) book a holiday
  B) buy a house
  C) seek advice on buying a product e.g. T.V. with satellite connection.

Example:

Getting help if pregnant

Preparation for group discussion: getting help if pregnant
Read:
→ Health leaflets
→ Internet sites

Summarise:
→ Sources of help e.g. your doctor, specialist agencies.
→ How to get them e.g. through an NHS clinic, your doctor.
→ Contact details e.g. telephone numbers, websites.

Make notes of:
→ The options.
→ The advantages and disadvantages of each option.
→ The important issues.
→ Ways of making decisions.

Taking part in a group discussion: getting help if pregnant
→ Listen to what others are saying.
→ Look at each person as they speak.
→ Answer questions.
→ Ask questions.
→ Make useful suggestions.

Examples of Short Talks you could give to practise and apply your skills:

- What I would do if I won the lottery.
- The advantages and disadvantages of marriage in the 21st Century.
- The Millennium Dome has been well worth all the money spent on it.
- Health and Safety in the workplace.

Example:

Advantages and Disadvantages of Marriage in the 21st Century

Preparation for a short talk: Marriage Yes or No
Read:
→ Books
→ Leaflets
→ Websites e.g. Government sites giving statistics on numbers of marriages and divorces.

Summarise:
→ Marriage and its meaning.
→ Types of marriage e.g. church or civil ceremonies.
→ The advantages e.g. level of commitment, tax benefits, financial security through to things like pensions.
→ The disadvantages e.g. religious aspects, level of commitment, the idea of modern relationships, divorce rates.

Plan your talk:
→ Who is the audience to be?
→ Use suitable images e.g. graphs of statistics, picture of a wedding.
→ What marriage means.
→ The advantages.
→ The disadvantages.
→ Marriage and divorce rates.
→ Length of marriages.
→ Summary.
→ Plan for questions.

Deliver your talk:
→ Speak clearly.
→ State your points.
→ Use images effectively.
→ Take questions.

Take feedback on your talk:
→ From the audience.
→ From your tutor/supervisor.
→ Carry out a self evaluation.

Communication Part B Tracking and Recording Sheets:

Tracking and Recording sheets

Communication Level 2 Part B C2.1 Discussions Take part in a discussion about a straightforward subject.	Evidence must show you can: <ul><li>Make clear and relevant contributions in a way that suits your purpose and situation.</li><li>Listen and respond appropriately to what others say.</li><li>Help to move the discussion forward.</li></ul>
I took part in a discussion with:	
Date of the discussion:	
The discussion was about:	
The purpose of the discussion was:	
I spoke clearly to make these points:	1 2 3
I listened to these points:	1 2 3
I asked these questions:	1 2 3
I moved the discussion forward by making these points:	1 2 3

Tracking and Recording sheets

Communication Level 2 Part B
C2.1 Discussions
Short Talk
Give a short talk about a straightforward subject, using an image.

Evidence must show you can:
- Speak clearly in a way that suits your subject, purpose and situation.
- Keep to the subject and structure your talk to help listeners follow what you are saying.
- Use an image to clearly illustrate your main points.

I gave a short talk about:

To people I know/don't know

Date of the talk:

The purpose of the talk was:

I spoke clearly to the audience to make these points:

1
2
3

I structured my talk, to make these points:

1
2
3

I used these images to make points:

1 Image:

    Point:

2 Image:

    Point:

Summary: Some common problems and solutions:

Summary

Problem	Solution
Not enough preparation.	Be very clear about the topic. Take enough time. Make good notes.
Speaking too much, gabbling or rushing.	Practise what you want to say before the discussion/talk. Do not interrupt.
Speaking too little.	Decide on one or two points that you will make. Practise what you want to say before the discussion/talk.
Speaking too softly or quietly.	Practise your talk, speaking it out loud to someone you know well.
Not listening to others.	It's easy to think that you have heard what someone has said, rather than what they did say. Focus on the speaker. Make notes if you need to. Try not to listen to what you want to hear.
Ignoring the views of others.	Do not get too excited or agitated by someone else's point of view. Remember – not everyone thinks the same as you. Try not to listen to what you want to hear. Do not attack people for their point of view, don't make it personal.

If you are having lots of problems, return to step one in Chapter 9. Check your checklists, go to the Help Desks and ask for advice if you need to, *before* you go on to the practice assignments.

2.2 Reading and Summarising

You could use any example of materials to read and summarise, but if you want to use the evidence in your portfolio, someone needs to record your skills as having met the criteria. You can help this process by keeping your own records and reflections of your reading using the tracking and recording sheets like those which follow on page 136. These sheets can be used to show how your skills are developing. They could also be part of your portfolio evidence to help show that you can use your skills in different situations.

Here are some examples of some topics for reading and summarising, to practise and apply your skills. In each case some possible source documents are given. Remember that you must be able to select your own material, from a given list, at level 2:

- The religion and customs of a culture different from your own.
  Sources: Encarta, CD-ROMs, books.
- A successful local business.
  Sources: newspapers, brochures, leaflets and fliers.
- A recent news issue.
  Sources: newspapers, magazines, library may source these on CD-ROM.
- Leisure facilities available for young people in your area.
  Sources: Local council records, leaflets, fliers, brochures, newspapers.

Help desk

Remember in each case you must have a purpose for your reading. This means that you must have a reason for reading. You must say why you need to get the information, and what you will use it for.

Example:

Flying Farriers – A successful local business

Decide:

→ What you will do with the information you find, choosing a suitable form and style e.g. article for a local newspaper.

→ What your sources will be (extended documents are needed at level 2) e.g. speaking to the farrier, business records, information from the local TEC.

→ What the key points and ideas are e.g. when the business started, how many people are employed, turnover, numbers of customers, increases in business each year, the specialised nature of the business, shoeing horses.

→ How to summarise the information e.g. start with a list of points, link them together, make the writing as short as possible for a newspaper article.

→ The images you will use e.g. business statistics as graphs.

Action:

→ Plan the layout of the article.

→ Decide where the images will be.

→ Produce a draft.

→ Proofread and check your work.

→ Get feedback on your work.

→ Produce the final version.

Communication Part B Tracking and Recording Sheets

Tracking and Recording sheets

Communication Level 2 Part B C2.2 Reading	Evidence must show you can:
Read and summarise information from two extended documents, about a straightforward subject including at least one image.	• Select and read relevant material. • Identify accurately the lines of reasoning and main points from text and images. • Summarise the information to suit your purpose.

I chose these documents to read:

1

2

I found information from at least two types of extended documents:

- Book ☐
- Magazine ☐
- Memo ☐
- Letter ☐
- Newspaper ☐
- Other ☐

I was trying to find out about:

The main points I found:

1	4
2	5
3	6
	7

The image I used was a :

Picture ☐
Chart ☐
Diagram ☐
Sketch ☐

The point made by the image was:

I used my summary for this purpose:

Summary: Some common problems and solutions:

Summary

Problems	Solutions
Not being able to decide which documents to read.	Make sure that you have clear instructions about the purpose of your reading.
Reading things which are not strictly relevant.	Scan and skim documents to pick out the main points, and get the gist of the content.
Choosing areas and points from your reading, which are not strictly needed.	Pick out key words and points as a list. Do not wander from the task/assignment. Understand what you are reading.
Summary is vague, too long or not clear.	Make short notes. Points must be specific. Put points in order. Understand your notes. Know what your notes are for: use in a discussion, to write a report.

If you are having lots of problems, return to step one in Chapter 9. Check your checklists, go to the Help Desks, and ask for advice if you need to, *before* you go on to the practice assignments.

2.3 Writing

You could use any example of writing, but if you want to use the evidence in your portfolio, someone needs to record your skills as having met the criteria. You can help this process by keeping your own records and reflections of your writing using tracking and recording sheets like those which follow on page 140. These sheets can be used to show how your skills are developing. They could also be part of your portfolio evidence, to help show that you can use your skills in different situations.

Here are some examples of some documents you could

write to practise and apply your skills. Remember that you have to decide what type of document to write at level 2. The examples here are to give you practice of writing different types of document:

- Essay on the advantages and disadvantages of genetic engineering (extended document).
- Information handout on a chosen career.
- Report on a local conservation project, which has been successfully completed (extended document).
- Poster advertising a concert for your favourite band.
- Report on the effects of increasing human populations, on world climate (extended document).
- A letter applying for a part-time job.
- Questionnaire for people of your age to find out their daily diet.

Example:

Information handout on a career as a Veterinary Nurse:

Veterinary Nurse
Qualifications required:
→ 5 GCSEs at A*–C, including English and Maths/Science.

Age at which you can begin:
→ 17

Relevant experience:
→ Work experience with a vet, experience with animals e.g. on a farm, in a kennels, cattery or stables.

Personal qualities:
→ Willing to work with, and be caring towards, people and animals; prepared to get your hands dirty, not worried about blood and gore; good spoken communication skills; well organised, good record keeper.

How to apply:
→ Get a place at college, or a pre-veterinary nursing course, if you are only 16, and train on the job through placement at an approved training centre.

A day in the life of:
→ Get involved in admitting patients for the day's operations. Take case histories; weights and measurements; calculate and administer pre-medication by injection; take blood samples; observations of behaviour.
→ Help the vet during consultations, getting equipment out, holding patients during treatments.
→ Assist the vet during operations, keep checking the anaesthetic machine.
→ Check stool samples of dog for worm eggs, and identify which type of worm.
→ Give treatments to animals as part of post-operative care.

→ Clean out kennels of patients.

→ Remove stitches, change dressings, check wounds at own clinic.

→ Run puppy socialisation classes on Tuesday evenings.

→ Check drug and equipment stores and re-order.

Training:

→ Veterinary Nursing qualification.

Career developments:

→ Can train in specific fields, such as medicine or surgery, for a diploma, or can become a pet health counsellor e.g. in dietary management.

Hours, holidays and benefits:

→ Depends on the vet you work for, but should get four weeks holiday; hours include evenings, some weekends, night-time on-call, and shift work.

Salary:

→ £13,000–£16,000 when qualified, some increase with experience and if managing other staff.

Communication Part B Tracking and Recording Sheets

Tracking and Recording sheets

Communication Level 2 Part B C2.3 Writing	Evidence must show you can:
Write two different types of documents about straightforward subjects. One piece of writing should be extended, and include one image.	• Present relevant information in an appropriate form. • Use a structure and style of writing to suit your purpose. • Ensure text is legible, and that spelling, punctuation and grammar are accurate, so your meaning is clear.

Document 1

Type of document I wrote:

Letter ☐
Memo ☐
Application form ☐
Notes ☐
Report ☐
Essay ☐

The image I have used is:

The structure and style of document 1 is......................
....
because...............................
....

I have checked my work for spelling, punctuation and grammar
Yes ☐   No ☐

I have changed my work to make sure that it can be easily read by others, and that the meaning is clear
Yes ☐   No ☐

Your signature:
Assessor signature:

Document 2

Type of document I wrote:

Letter ☐
Memo ☐
Application form ☐
Notes ☐
Report ☐
Essay ☐

The image I have used is:

The structure and style of document 2 is......................
....
because...............................
....

I have checked my work for spelling, punctuation and grammar
Yes ☐   No ☐

I have changed my work to make sure that it can be easily read by others, and that the meaning is clear
Yes ☐   No ☐

Date:

DEFINITIONS ▶

Extended document is one that is at least three pages long, see Chapter 9 for further explanation.

Summary: Some common problems and solutions:

Summary

Problem	Solution
Writing too much, and waffling.	Stick to your list of points. Write in short, clear sentences.
Not using an appropriate style.	Make sure that you understand the task or assignment set, before you begin.
Not structuring work sensibly.	Put your points into order. Use headings and paragraphs to help. Make suitable connections between parts of your work.
Not using images sensibly.	Choose a picture, graph or chart only if it supports a point which you want to make.
Not proofreading and correcting.	Use a dictionary or spell checker. Check that the basic rules of grammar and punctuation have been applied.

If you are having lots of problems, return to step one in Chapter 9. Check your checklists, go to the Help Desks and ask for advice if you need to, *before* you go on to the next set of practice tasks and assignments.

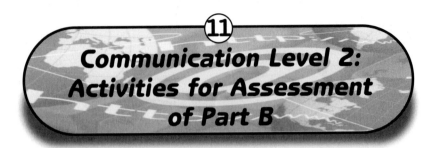

Communication Level 2: Activities for Assessment of Part B

Portfolio Assignments Level 2

These are further examples from different situations, which can be used as portfolio evidence to meet Part B of the unit requirements. Some of the examples focus on one component of Communication, others are larger, combined assignments.

In Communication you can evidence each component separately, or together.

You should not try to separate the criteria within each component e.g. when you take part in a discussion, you must show that you have:

Made clear, relevant contributions
AND
Listened and responded appropriately
AND
Helped to move the discussion forward.

Help desk

Communication unit: Part B

Has four components or parts at level 2.	C2.1a Discussions C2.1b Short Talk C2.2 Reading C2.3 Writing These four parts can be evidenced separately, or together.
Each component or part has three criteria. Example: C2.1a Discussions	• Make clear and relevant contributions in a way that suits your purpose and situation. • Listen and respond appropriately to what others say. • Help to move the discussion forward.

These three criteria should not be separated when you produce evidence of your discussion for your portfolio.

There are ideas below for activities which are designed to evidence separately:

1) Discussions

2) Short Talks

3) Reading

4) Writing

There are activities involving:

1) Reading and discussion

2) Reading and short talk

3) Reading and writing

There are activities involving:

1) Discussion, short talk, reading and writing.

2.1a Discussions

• Take part in a group discussion on the importance of labelling foods which contain GMOs.

- Take part in a group discussion about an environmental issue.
- Take part in a group discussion about getting help and information about sexual harassment.
- Take part in a mock interview for a job.
- Review a film you have seen recently and take part in a discussion about it.
- Prepare for a discussion with your supervisor/tutor about the courses you hope to take after your GCSEs. Take part in the discussion and evaluate your performance.
- You have a part-time job. The hours you work have been arranged around your school/college timetable and study time. Now your employer wants you to work more hours each week, and has said that if you cannot do this, you will be sacked. Take part in a discussion about how to deal with this situation.

2.1b Short Talk

- Give a short talk about your most recent holiday.
- Give a short talk about your pet.
- Give a short talk about the health and safety arrangements at your work placement/local business.
- Give a short talk about one aspect of your work that you enjoy.
- Give a short talk about a piece of coursework/assignment.

2.2 Reading and Summarising

- Prepare a summary of the benefits available to unemployed people.
- Prepare a summary on local leisure facilities, ready to use in a poster, for young people.

2.3 Writing

- Write an account of a foreign holiday, as a diary (extended document).
- Write an information leaflet about a local zoo, wildlife centre, theme park, or other attraction.
- Write an article for a magazine or newsletter, about a local community event, such as a sponsored walk, sporting event, concert or amateur dramatic production.
- Write an up to date C.V. (curriculum vitae) as part of your personal career planning and preparation for courses post-16.

Help desk

C.V. means a summary of:

Your personal details, such as name, address.

Your qualifications.

Details of your education record, such as which schools you attended.

Your other experiences, and responsibilities, such as outdoor pursuits, being a prefect, being a team captain.

Your hobbies and interests, and sporting activities.

Example CV:

Name: Winston Smith

Address: 10 The Flats, Weald Way, Weald, N. Essex. WE0 0NE

Qualifications:

GCSE grades achieved in 2000

English Language C

English Spoken 2

Mathematics D

Science C,C

History B

French C

Geography D

CDT Design B

Education:

Weald High School, Weald, N. Essex. WE3 3NE

Responsibilities: Library assistant, football team captain, quiz team captain.

Additional experience:

Work experience placement for three weeks at local council offices; clerical assistant in a local solicitors in year 11.

Part-time job, for 10 hours per week, 1998–2000, at B&B DIY store, helping customers.

School football tours 1997–2000, to N. England, Midlands and Holland.

Hobbies and interests:

Football, swimming and cricket. I also like to do DIY projects, and have made wooden cabinets, and furniture at home. In school I worked in a team of four to design a piece of equipment to help someone who cannot move around very well. This was part of a Young Designers project, and we came third in Britain for our motorised scooter design.

2.1a, 2.2 Reading and discussion

- Research the climate and geography of another culture. Take part in a group discussion about your findings.

2.1b, 2.2 Reading and short talk

- Research the costs of 'changing rooms' for a one-bedroom flat. Your budget is £500, and you have to redecorate the flat. Give a short talk explaining your plans for the flat, using at least one image.

2.2, 2.3 Reading and writing

- Plan and budget for an activity holiday with a group of friends. Prepare a written plan and costing for your holiday.
- Find out about the costs of living away from home, and write an information sheet for 16–19 year olds, who may want to leave home.
- Research the employment and education opportunities open to you. Fill in an application form for a job.
- Research the costs of private health care which are available. Prepare a report which summarises your findings.
- Plan and budget for a school disco. Take into account costs of hiring a hall and a disco. Work out how much you have to charge people to cover your costs.
- Compare the costs of running a car and a motorbike. Take into account tax, insurance and fuel costs. Choose a particular make and model of car and motorbike. Write your findings in a table.

2.1a, 2.1b, 2.2, 2.3 Discussion, short talk, reading and writing

- Research recycling facilities in your area; discuss your ideas in a group. Make a presentation of your findings as a display for a local library, or in your school or college. Make your display as visually appealing as possible. Prepare a short talk to go with your presentation.
- Research the ways in which a particular food is advertised in newspapers, magazines, on radio and TV. Discuss your findings. Give a short talk on your findings to a group of people. Write a summary of your findings to be used as part of a written assignment.

Help desk

Recycling facilities in S. E. Kent

1) Plan your activity, with the steps you need to take, and amount of time needed.

2) Identify your sources of information e.g. local council, library.

3) Say what information you chose and why.

4) Pick out key points and ideas e.g. what can be recycled, and where?

5) Make notes on your findings e.g. as a list or table.

6) Summarise your findings as preparation for your talk.

7) Plan the talk e.g. what points will you make, in which order, using which images?

8) Give the talk, and take feedback on your performance.

9) Plan the article for the newsletter e.g. what format will it have, who will read it, how long will it be, what images will you use?

10) Draft, proofread, and change if necessary.

11) Produce the final version.

12 Communication Level 2: Putting Your Portfolio Together for Part B

Introduction

This part of the book will help you to plan your assignments, and your portfolio, to meet Part B of the Communication unit. This section also has some record sheets, to help you plan and track your progress. You can use any of the ideas and examples in the first parts of the book to provide evidence. Remember that the contexts in which you developed your skills for Part A should be different to those used to show the application of your skills, for Part B. Your portfolio examples should not be re-worked or rehearsed tasks, but they show you can build on what you have learned, and that you can apply your skills in new situations.

Planning

This is the process of:

- Taking the set task or assignment.
- Dividing it up into small steps.
- Keeping it in a timescale.
- Putting it in a sensible order.

The planning process is needed if you are to structure your work, and do it in a logical order. It will help you keep to deadlines, so you do not have to rush at the end. Look at the Action Plan below:

Action Plan:

Task or assignment title:	
What are your action Steps? Who will help you?	Target dates for completion:
Part B Communication evidence produced: 2.1a	Dates completed:
2.1b	
2.2	
2.3	
IT evidence:	
Application of Number evidence:	
Your signature:	Date:
Assessor signature:	

Review and check progress

Regularly check back to your plan, to see what you have achieved and what is left. Are you sticking to time? Are you working in order? What is going well and what is difficult? See the table below.

Review:

First review:	Date:
With:	Name of assessor:
Which action steps have you completed?	Action taken:
What has gone well?	
What has been difficult?	
Any changes made to your plan?	
What feedback have you been given?	
Which action steps remain/new action steps?	Dates:
What have you achieved?	
Part B Communication evidence produced:	Dates completed:
2.1a	
2.1b	
2.2	
2.3	
IT evidence:	
Application of Number evidence:	
Date of next review:	
Your signature:	Date:
Assessor signature:	

Using your Communication Skills to best advantage:

Performance checklist:

Check that you have:

Planned your group discussion.

Structured your work.

Planned your short talk.

Written and re-written your work until you are satisfied that it is as good as it can be.

Planned your reading to make best use of the sources of information.

Written a memo.

Written an application form.

Made good notes of the main points.

Written a letter:

Written an essay:

Written a summary:

Written a report:

Help desk

Feedback:

Using feedback to improve your work:

You should get regular feedback from your teacher/supervisor. This should be specific with targets for improvement. You should know what you have completed and what you have left to do. Any work not yet finished should be listed with new completion dates.

Portfolio Record Sheet Level 2

- Use the sheet below to record your portfolio evidence. This should be evidence from tasks, assignments and problem-solving activities to cover Part B of the unit. The evidence must reach the standard set out in the Communication unit.
- Your teacher/assessor/supervisor must agree with you that your evidence reaches the required standard. Remember the contexts recorded here should be different from those used above, to practise and develop your skills for Part A.

For example:

→ You could use the same activity for several components of the unit, or you could use different activities for each part.

→ You could find out about the options available to you in education, post-16 (C2.2), and discuss it with your tutor (C2.1a)
→ You could write a summary of your findings for other people to use (C2.3).
→ You could take part in a group discussion about drug abuse (C2.1a).
→ You could find out about job opportunities locally (C2.2).
→ You could write a short essay about the way people use their leisure time locally (C2.3).

You will also find that larger activities and tasks will provide opportunities for combined evidence, which can also be used as part of your Application of Number and IT portfolios.

Remember, do not try to separate the criteria within each component. When you produce some writing, for example, your written evidence must:

Present relevant information in a suitable form

AND

Use a suitable style and structure for your purpose

AND

Demonstrate that your spelling, punctuation and grammar is accurate.

Tracking and Recording sheets

Communication	Activity I took part in:	Evidence in my portfolio:	Page Number(s)	Date
Part B **2.1a Discussions**				
Group				
Straightforward subject				
2.1b Short talk Lasting 5–6 minutes Familiar audience of 2–3 Straightforward subject Use image(s)		Image:		
2.2 Reading and Summarising Information from two extended documents, including image(s) Straightforward subject		Image: Document 1: Document 2:		
2.3 Writing Document 1 on a straightforward subject.				
2.3 Writing Document 2, extended, on a straightforward subject, with image(s).		Image:		

Portfolio-Building Level 2

The portfolio must show that you have all the skills set out in Part B of the unit. It should show that you can apply your skills in a variety of different situations. Look at the box below for guidance.

- Set up your portfolio at the very beginning.
- Divide the portfolio into: 1) Units
                               2) Components or parts.
- Listen to the guidance given by your teacher/supervisor.
- Remember it is *quality* not *quantity* which is important.
- Choose examples of evidence which prove your skills and knowledge beyond any doubt.
- Do not be afraid to replace early examples of work with better ones from later in your course.
- It is a good idea to include rough or first drafts of a piece of work, labelled as such, with the final version. This shows that this is your own work, and that you planned and developed your ideas.
- Put the unit specifications at level 2 in the front.
- Include a contents page at the front, which shows the Key Skills units included, and the order of the work.
- Put an index at the start of each Key Skills unit, showing where each piece of evidence can be found.
- Number all the pages. This is the easiest way for anyone to find individual pieces of evidence. It also means that you can use one piece of evidence to meet the requirements of more than one unit.
- Use portfolio records to list your evidence, and to show which part(s) of the standards it meets.

Level 2 Portfolio example layout

Contents page

Name:

Organisation:

Key Skills Units and Levels: Include the Communication Level 2 specifications.

Section 1: Pages 1–26: Communication Level 2.

Section 2: Pages 27–53: Application of Number Level 2.

Section 3: Pages 54–71: IT Level 2.

Index for Communication Level 2.

Examples of evidence for a Level 2 Communication Portfolio

Page 1: Completed Portfolio Record Sheet

Pages 2–5: 2.1a Discussions: Group

Pages 2–4: Notes of discussion with my group about post-16 options.

Page 5: Observation checklist completed by teacher/supervisor.

Pages 6–12: 2.1b Short talk
        Pages 6–8 Notes from reading about my hobby/interest.
        Page 9 List of the main points in the talk, in order.
        Page 10 Questions asked and my answers.
        Page 11 Feedback sheets from the audience.
        Page 12 Observation checklist completed by my teacher/supervisor.

Pages 13–16: 2.2 Reading
        Page 13 The assignment brief with list of chapters, and articles I read.
        Pages 13–15 The notes I made.
        Page 16 The list of books, chapters and sections I used, with reasons.

Pages 17–21: 2.3 Writing
        Document 1: The notes and summary sheet on types of food eaten by people in my organisation.

Pages 22–26: 2.3 Writing
        Document 2 The report for my assignment on the survey of mobile phone use by people in my organisation.

Communication Level 3: Developing the Skills and Knowledge in Part A

Introduction

This part of the book will help you to develop and practise your Communication skills as set out in Part A of the unit at level 3. It will also help you get ready for the test at level 3 which is based mainly on Part A.

Remember that at level 3 you need to be able to do everything at level 2, and the extra things at level 3. If you find any of this section difficult, and need more help, look in the level 2 section.

When speaking, listening, reading and writing, it is important to think about:

What you want to say:

What are the important facts, opinions, or points, which you want to make? Are you trying to explain or describe something?

Why you want to say it:

What is the reason for speaking, reading or writing and what do you intend to achieve? Are you discussing something? Do you want to argue a point of view? Are you giving information?

Who you are speaking or writing to:

How will you know that your style and approach is appropriate? Is it formal enough? What is the setting? Who, and how many people are in your audience?

DEFINITIONS ▶

Key Skills Words: Complex

At level 3 you need to be able to deal with complex subjects, ideas and issues by making sense of several interconnected parts of say an argument, so that the view you present can be understood by others. You could also deal with a subject, idea or issue in a complex way, perhaps by demonstrating a sensitive approach to the subject.

For example: You could describe what happened at an event, such as a political rally (not complex). You could explain the political motivation and expectations resulting from speeches given at a political rally (complex). You could present the view of a political party, as expressed at a rally about a sensitive issue, such as the banning of fox hunting (complex).

Discussions (Speaking and Listening)

DEFINITIONS ▶

Key Skills Words: Discussion

At level 3 this should be a group discussion, and must be about a complex subject.

Checklist: When preparing for a discussion:

- Know the topic.
- Know the purpose.
- Know your own role.
- Make notes.
- Try to think of some questions that you could ask others. The questions should be helpful and positive.

Checklist: When taking part in any discussion:

- Make sure that you understand the reason for the discussion.
- The role of those taking part.
- Know who is leading the discussion.
- Speak clearly, using words everyone can understand.
- Make relevant points, give specific examples of what you mean.
- Ask suitable questions. Try to ask an open question, which allows others to respond.
- Show by your body language that you are listening.
- Listen for the tone of people's voices, and the type of language used (vocabulary).
- Watch their gestures.
- Try to understand their point of view.
- Summarise what has been said, to check that everyone has the same understanding.
- Enlarge and develop what has been said, or agreed.
- Encourage others to develop their point of view.
- Acknowledge differences of opinion in a sensitive way.
- Consider the feelings of other people, when you contribute.
- Change the way you take part to suit the situation and your purpose, such as: presenting your ideas, expressing an opinion or describing events.

ACTIVITY:

You are taking part in a discussion, as part of an AS General Studies or other course, about stereotyping and discrimination in our society. You have each been asked to research examples of groups of people, of which there are stereotyped images, e.g. the elderly, women, young men, black people. Try to find examples of discrimination against these groups of people. Is this acceptable in a modern society?

How do you prepare for, and take part in, this discussion?

Go through the checklists:

- Be prepared:
→ Know who you are speaking to, and when.
→ Know how much time you have for the discussion.
→ Take your notes with you.
→ Know which of your points are most important to say, for the purpose of the discussion.

- Take part:
→ Listen carefully to what others say.
→ Ask helpful, open questions, which allow others to contribute.
→ Summarise points, check you have understood what has been said.
→ Write notes if you need to.
→ Agree what is to be done, by you and others, and by when.

Help desk

Preparation and notes which could be used for the discussion above on stereotyping

Prepare by finding suitable sources:
→ Select useful documents and say why they are useful.
→ Reading, skimming and scanning.

Make notes of:
→ your findings, ideas and views, based on the information.
→ identify groups of people.
→ what is the stereotype of each group?
→ what is it based on e.g. anecdote, example, bias, prejudice?
→ examples of discrimination against these groups in British society e.g. career opportunities for women; the numbers of senior managers in business who are female/black/over 40/disabled; state funding for church schools of different religions.
→ Consider the acceptability of discrimination, e.g. is it fair; is it morally acceptable; is it good for business or the country as a whole; does it lead to violence, anti-social behaviour, or yob-culture?

Make your points during the discussion e.g.:
→ 'There are stereotypes of many groups of people including....'
→ 'I have found the stereotype for disabled people to be based on prejudice, and lack of empathy for other people'
→ 'I have found an example of discrimination against women'
→ 'I do not think discrimination against groups of people is right, because it leads others to be violent towards them.'

Help desk

Open Questions

These allow other people to give their own opinion, and are valuable during discussions, because they move things forward. Open questions develop ideas and allow others to join in:
e.g. 'What do you think about…?'.
'Why do you think that happened?'

Closed Questions

Usually need 'Yes' or 'No' answers, or one-word replies:
e.g. 'What day is it today?'.
'Do you want to go to the cinema?'
They are not very helpful in discussions, as they do not encourage people to give their own view or opinion.

In summary: Some Do's and Don'ts:

DO'S ✓

Make notes of the points you want to make.

Speak clearly, using suitable language.

Be able to give information, or present an argument clearly.

Listen to others, and show you are listening.

Make eye contact.

Ask several relevant, open questions.

Ask someone to make their point more clearly, or to enlarge upon their point.

Summarise what has been said as you understand it.

Be sensitive to the opinions and feelings of others.

DON'TS ✗

Be unprepared.
Use slang or jargon.
Be too loud, or too quiet.
Be unsympathetic to what others say.
Ignore others.
Interrupt the person speaking.
Answer without being sure of what the person asked.
Assume that you understand how someone else feels.
Make your arguments complicated, or difficult for others to follow.

Giving a Presentation

When preparing to give a presentation:
- Research the topic thoroughly.
- Know the purpose.
- Know the audience. How many? Who are they?
- Plan appropriately to the needs of the audience.
- How formal or complex should you be, what is a suitable style?
- Are you presenting an argument, a solution to a problem, or reporting on an event?
- Make notes, this will give the structure of your talk.
- Include some relevant examples, stories or statistics.
- Choose a few pictures, models, or diagrams to make your points.
- Plan time for questions, and think through what you might be asked.
- Practise your talk by actually saying it out loud.

When giving a presentation:
- Use your notes to help you.
- Try to introduce the topic with an interesting fact, or a story.
- Make sure that your presentation has an introduction, a middle and an end.
- Keep looking at your audience, not just at the person in front of you.
- Speak clearly, and loudly enough for people at the back to hear.
- Use gestures to emphasise points.
- Engage your audience with relevant examples, stories or anecdotes.
- Vary the tone of your voice to give emphasis.

- Use a picture, chart or model to make a point.
- Demonstrate how to do something.
- Pass something around for people to look at.
- Look for signs that people do not understand, or are bored, and respond appropriately.
- Allow time for questions, or to explain points again.

ACTIVITY:

You have been asked to give a short presentation on the findings of your project, completed as part of a recent AS/A2 level Biology/Geography/Geology/PE or other residential activity. You have a maximum of 10 minutes, to explain:

1) the title of your project.

2) the methods you chose and why.

3) your findings and the presentation of your findings (use at least one image).

4) your evaluation of the project.

How do you prepare for and give this presentation?

Go through the checklists:

- Be prepared:
→ Know who you are speaking to, and when.
→ Know how much time you have for the presentation.
→ Take your notes with you.
→ Know which of your points are most important to say, and in what order.
→ Structure your presentation carefully to make it easy to follow.
→ Prepare for questions you think may be asked.

Example

Help desk

Presentation of findings from Biology field course

Title: The number of air bladders along the length of the seaweed, *Ascophyllum nodosum*, does not change in the lower, middle and upper shore.

Practical methods: The method involves:
→ Finding the lower, middle and upper zones of the shore.
→ Measuring the lengths of 50 fronds of Ascophyllum in each zone, in cm, with a metre rule.
→ Counting the number of air bladders in each of the 50 fronds in each zone.
→ Recording the data in a table:

TABLE RECORDING DATA ON Ascophyllum nodosum					
ZONE OF SHORE	LOWER		MIDDLE		UPPER	
Sample Fronds	Length in cm	Number of Bladders	Length in cm	Number of Bladders	Length in cm	Number of Bladders
1	186	60	154	36	100	18
2	178	74	144	32	90	17
3	190	64	139	40	80	14
4	and so on ...					

Findings:
→ The length of *Ascophyllum* frond increases from the upper to the lower shore.
→ The number of air bladders increases from the upper to the lower shore.
→ The ratio of bladders to length increases from the upper to the lower shore.

TABLE OF FINDINGS ON Ascophyllum nodosum (continued)

ZONE OF SHORE	LOWER	MIDDLE	UPPER
SAMPLE FRONDS	RATIO OF LENGTH: NO OF BLADDERS	RATIO OF LENGTH: NO OF BLADDERS	RATIO OF LENGTH: NO OF BLADDERS
1	0.32	0.23	0.18
2	0.42	0.36	0.19
3	0.34	0.28	0.18
4	and so on ...		

Evaluation of the methods and findings:

→ Methods were simple to use in the field.
→ Tables for recording data and calculations were prepared before going into the field.
→ The location of the shore is Angle Bay, S. Wales.
→ This is a sheltered shore, with good populations of Ascophyllum in each zone.
→ Data collected is evaluated as statistically valid since the sample sizes of 50 in each zone are large.
→ The proportion of air bladders increases from the top to the bottom of the shore.

Conclusions and Explanation:

→ The length of fronds increases in the lower shore because the height of water is greatest here when the tide is in.
→ There are more bladders per length of seaweed in the lower shore to help the longer lengths float in a greater depth of water.
→ This is necessary to allow the Ascophyllum to photosynthesise effectively while submerged in a large depth of water.
→ Photosynthesis can only take place when the seaweed is submerged.

Help desk

Four P's for successful presentations		
Plan	Prepare	Practice
For **Perfect** Performance		
Remember the more prepared and practised you are the better you will feel, and the better it will go.		

In summary: Some Do's and Don'ts:

DO'S ✓

Be prepared and practised.

Use your plan and follow it.

Present your ideas and points in a sensible order.

Use standard English.

Breathe deeply and regularly, to help stay calm if you are nervous.

Wait for the audience to be quiet.

Smile sometimes.

Use gestures for emphasis.

Keep going even if you forget something or miss something out.

Use pictures, plans or diagrams to help.

Be enthusiastic about the topic.

Engage the audience with stories, or interesting facts.

Use humour to help engage the audience.

DON'TS X

Read from your notes without looking up.

Be afraid to repeat what you say, if people do not understand.

Use slang or jargon.

Rush through your talk.

Speak in the same boring tone.

Speak over the audience.

Look frightened.

Move about, fidget, or wave your hands, too much.

Don't say 'um' or 'er' too much.

Use images unless the whole audience can see them, and benefit from them.

Make rude or prejudiced jokes.

Reading and Synthesising:

When finding different sources:

- Use the library, databases, and the Internet to find your sources of reference.
- Use the contents pages.
- Use the indexes to look up key words.
- Select the materials you are using and say why each is useful.
- Use a range of sources to give different opinions, supporting data or ideas.
- Be prepared to research some aspects further, to gain more understanding.

DEFINITIONS ▶

Extended document means at least three pages long. You must use at least two extended documents as your sources for your portfolio evidence. This is a guide, but means about three pages of text.

When skimming, scanning and reading:

- Skim books, articles, reports and secondary sources to get the gist of them.
- Scan materials to pick out the main points and ideas.
- Read the relevant sections in detail.

When identifying the type of document and its purpose:

- Recognise the format of the material. Is it a formal letter or memo?

- Recognise the writer's purpose or intention. Is he/she presenting an argument? Are opinions given? Is it biased?
- What is the line of reasoning being followed? Look for the facts and evidence being presented. What conclusions are being drawn? Look for repetition confirming an idea, and examples used to support the reasoning, such as facts, statistics and quotations.
- Look for the tone of writing, and types of words used. Is it a factual report, or a set of instructions?
- Pick out the main points from the text and from images.

DEFINITIONS ▶

When following an argument or line of reasoning:

There should be a sequence of key points in logical order, which it is possible to follow as the reader.

Each key point should be explored and developed, and repeated using different words.

Each key point should be supported with examples and evidence.

When synthesising information:

- Pick out the key words and meaning.
- Put them into sentences.
- Plan your own work to present a coherent argument or sequence of events.
- Put your account together which includes your own interpretation of the information and can be used for a presentation, report or an essay.

DEFINITIONS ▶

At level 3 you have to present your own views, opinions and perspective, taken from the work of other people, or from your own original research. Synthesising is about combining ideas into a whole and complex argument, proposal, presentation or theory.

ACTIVITY:

You have been asked to research the arguments for and against genetically modified foods, both in the short-term and the long-term. You will need to present your findings in your own words, by synthesising key information, and presenting it in a suitable and appropriate form.

Example:

```
(Help)desk
```

Report on the arguments for and against GM foods in the short- and long-term

Sources used with reasons:
→ Government publications, websites e.g. Ministry of Agriculture, Food and Fisheries – to give current information on Government concerns, controls and restrictions, should have relatively unbiased information.
→ Publications, websites of environmental pressure groups e.g. Friends of the Earth, Greenpeace – to give the view of those opposed to GM foods, environmental concerns, may have information unavailable on Government sites.
→ Publications, websites of Biotechnology companies developing GM foods e.g. British Biotech, Monsanto – to give the view of those for GM foods, the benefits and advantages.

The format and style for presenting findings:
→ Present as a report, with heading above.
→ Make key points, based on sources.
→ Acknowledge bias in sources.
→ Synthesise ideas into coherent arguments for and against.
→ Use headings/sub-headings, bullet points.

Headings/sub-headings:
→ Advantages of GM foods:
→ Short-term
→ Long-term
→ Disadvantages of GM foods:
→ Short-term
→ Long-term
→ Government controls:
→ To make GM foods safer
→ To improve access to information on GM foods.

Key points and issues in sensible order:
→ Use headings as the basis for the order.
→ Advantages include: pest-resistant crops; drought-resistant crops; greater food production; more land available for cultivation; cheaper; healthier food with more nutrients, edible vaccines against disease, reduced use of chemicals.
→ Disadvantages include: environmental contamination of other crops;

reduction of the gene pool; reduced biodiversity; exploitation of food animals; long-term effects on health; increased use of chemicals; some effects are unknown, including combined effects.
→ Government controls and rules include: labelling foods and ingredients; field testing; codes of practice; monitoring effects; limiting size of GM crops; research into the effects.

Synthesis of key points and issues:
→ Outline the advantages of GM foods in terms of: increased food production for a growing human population especially in areas of famine or drought; improved quality of food; needing less space to grow in already crowded world; reduction in the use of herbicides benefits everyone, cheaper for farmers, better for wildlife and the environment.
→ Outline the disadvantages of GM foods in terms of: potential damage to the environment due to reduction of biodiversity; contamination of crops by cross-pollination; increased health risks from eating combinations of GM products in the long-term.
→ Outline Government controls and rules on labelling: improve labelling requirements, so that everyone can choose to eat GM foods or not; funding for research into long-term and combined effects on health and the environment; regulation, monitoring and limitation on amount grown; code of practice to improve standards and practices.

In summary: Some Do's and Don'ts:

DO'S ✓

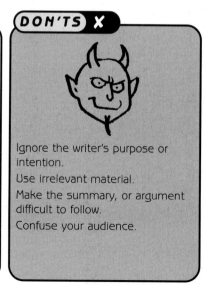

Skim, scan, read.
Use references.
Use contents and index pages.
Identify your main points.
Structure your summary.
Synthesise the information to give your own views and interpretation of the information.

DON'TS X

Ignore the writer's purpose or intention.
Use irrelevant material.
Make the summary, or argument difficult to follow.
Confuse your audience.

Writing

Checklist: When writing:

Make sure that you know the layout for:

A memo:

- This is a way of giving information or instructions to one or more people in a work situation, or to record what has occurred.
- Put the heading 'Memo' or 'Memorandum' in large letters at the top.
- Say who it is to.
- Give the name(s) of anyone else to whom the memo is to be circulated as Copy Circulated (CC).
- Say who it is from.
- Give the date.
- State the subject of the memo.
- Make the memo short and to the point.

Example:

(**H e l p**) ***d e s k***

Memo

To: Brian, Bob, Sarah, Steve, Simon, Hilary
CC: Heather
From: Christine
4 Feb 2001

Equal Opportunities policy presentation: 10 February 2001, 10.00 a.m. in Room 12

This is to confirm that there will be a presentation of the company's newly updated equal opportunities policy, and the plan for implementation, for all staff at your level. This will take place as above. Any ideas or suggestions that you have to bring to the discussion during this meeting will be most welcome. The company is committed to evaluating current policies and practices, with a view to radical change, and a new approach, if necessary. This obviously includes a very complex set of issues in a company as large as ours, not least because we are a multi-site operation.

Refreshments will be available. Please bring your copy of the policy (attached). The meeting will end at 12 noon.

Thank you,
Christine

A business letter:

This is an example of a formal letter.

- Write this type of letter when applying for a job or grant, when writing to any organisation, including Government offices, making a complaint, requesting information or payment.
- Put your name and address in the top right-hand corner.
- Put the name and address of the person you are writing to, underneath, but on the left side of the page.
- Put the date underneath.
- Below the date, start the letter with: 'Dear Sir', 'Dear Madam' or 'Dear Ms Brown'.
- Use formal language, explaining clearly why you are writing.
- End the letter with 'Yours faithfully' if it started 'Dear Sir or Madam' or 'Yours sincerely' if it started with 'Dear Ms Brown'.
- Sign and print your name underneath.

Example:

Help desk

Padraig Malley
2 Glen Coe
Sheepley
Isle of Skye
W. Isles
Scotland
SK1 1SS

Jennifer Higgins
Wessex County Council
Learning and Education Services
PO Box 666
County Hall
Wessex
WM1 1DL

10 March 2001

Dear Ms Higgins,

I am writing to apply for the post of assistant librarian as advertised in the *Evening Gazette*, on 5 March 2001. I enclose the application form which you sent me, together with the equal opportunities monitoring form. Police check and membership of secret societies declarations are also enclosed as requested. Thank you for the information regarding this post, which I would very much like to take up, should I be give the opportunity.

I am currently in my second year of Advanced level studies, and I feel that I have developed my skills of organisation and planning considerably this year. I enjoy helping people, and being able to guide them to the information they need. I have also greatly developed my IT skills by working in the library at school.

As you can see in my application form, I have been school librarian for three years now, and have been able to take much more responsibility for the day-to-day running of the library since being in the sixth form. I have been able to work effectively with a team of year 10 library assistants, and have explained to them the cataloguing and referencing system we have in use. I also did my work experience in the local library last year.

I hope you will find that my skills and experience make me a suitable candidate for this post, and look forward to hearing from you. If you require any further information, please do not hesitate to contact me.

Yours sincerely,

Padraig Malley

An informal letter, personal note or e-mail to a friend:
This is to someone you know well.
- The language should be informal and friendly.
- You can use slang and jargon familiar to you both.
- You can use humour and jokes, and present your writing much more as you would speak.

Example:

Help desk

Dear Ida,

Thanks for the brilliant email from your latest destination, Portugal. After so long in Ecuador, it must be weird. How are you finding the food, people, wine, driving, work etc.? I've never been there, so I look forward to coming to visit.
When can I come? Do you have any holidays soon?

I have started checking out flights, and so far there are plenty every day, depends where you want to fly from (which affects cost quite a bit).
What is your new flat like? If it's small I can stay in a B&B, or whatever they call them over there. At least it's a short flight not like 10 hours to S. America!
Really looking forward to seeing you,
Cheers,
Sian

An application form:

- Write in capitals or type, so that your words are very clear.
- Give the facts about yourself, and your experience.
- Do not make things up.
- Be as positive as you can about the things you can do.

Example:

Wessex County Council

Application form

Complete this form in block capitals.

Personal details:

Last name:

First names:

Address:

Telephone number:

Date of birth:

Place of birth:

Nationality:

Education:

Secondary (give details including qualifications obtained)

Dates: School/College: Qualifications:

Further/Higher education (give details including qualifications obtained)

Dates: University/College: Qualifications:

Employment History:

Give details of employment history in reverse chronological order, including responsibilities and descriptions of duties.

Dates: Employer name and address:

Additional information:

List any other courses and qualifications taken or about to be taken.

Give details of any relevant experience you have had e.g. community or volunteer work.

Interests and activities including voluntary work, clubs, hobbies and sport.

Supplementary information:

Summarise your strengths and weaknesses in applying for this position.

References:

Give details of two referees, one of whom should be your current or most recent employer.

Signature:

Date:

A report:

This could be an account of an event:

- Describe what has happened.
- Explain where it happened.
- Say why it happened.
- State who was part of the event.
- Use a heading and subheadings
- This could give technical information.
- Make points, use numbers or bullets where sensible.
- Describe a piece of equipment, or a process.

Example:

Help desk

Report on an environmental issue: Global Warming

Global warming is a term which refers to the increase in the temperature of the earth, not over many thousands of years, as has happened numerous times in its history, but in 10 or 20 years. Many scientists and environmental campaigners believe that global warming is taking place rapidly, mainly due to human activities.

The causes of global warming

The burning of fossil fuels produces carbon dioxide, as does the respiration of organisms. The amount of carbon dioxide produced during respiration is used up by green plants as they photosynthesise. The additional carbon dioxide, produced by burning fossil fuels, is accumulating in the atmosphere, leading to a rise in its level. This increase in carbon dioxide levels may be preventing the sun's heat from leaving the earth, causing temperatures to rise.

The Greenhouse effect

The action of the increased carbon dioxide levels in the atmosphere is similar to that of a greenhouse holding the heat in, in the same way that glass does. Other gases, whose levels have increased recently, and are known to cause this effect include:

- CFCs
- Methane
- Nitrous oxide

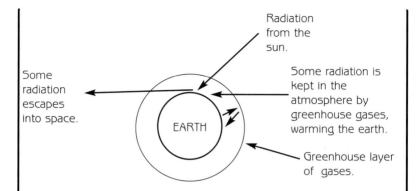

The possible effects of global warming

The greenhouse effect may lead to serious consequences, including:

→ Melting of polar ice caps.

→ Rising sea level.

→ Flooding of coastal areas, including many cities.

→ Changing rainfall and climate patterns.

→ Changing plant and animal populations as some species die out.

→ Changing habitats and ecosystems.

→ Increasing numbers of pest and disease causing organisms.

Alternative theories

→ Variations in the intensity of the sun are causing changes.

→ The temperature of the world is increasing naturally as it leaves the most recent ice age.

→ There has always been a greenhouse effect, because of the gases naturally found in the earth's atmosphere.

This is an example of a short report for a school magazine or newspaper, covering a complex issue.

An essay:

This is one way to answer a question, write an assignment, or perhaps a piece of coursework.

● The most important thing is to answer the question.

● Plan your essay so that it has a beginning, a middle, and an end.

● Write a rough draft after your plan.

● The rough draft has key points, key words, your basic ideas, the order of your essay.

● Write clearly, in sentences.

● Use paragraphs to divide the essay into sections: beginning, middle and end.

Example:

```
Help desk
```

Essay title: *The Work of Charles Darwin and the results of his theories*

Charles Darwin was born in Shrewsbury, on 12 February 1809. His father Robert Darwin was a doctor, who wanted his son to become a doctor. His mother was from the family of the famous potter, Josiah Wedgwood. She died when Charles was only 8 years old. He showed no interest in medicine, but he was always a great collector, starting as a boy, when he collected insects and shells.

In August 1831, two Cambridge professors that he knew wrote to Darwin inviting him to join HMS Beagle as official naturalist, during a voyage to explore South America. These invitations eventually led to Darwin's theories on evolution being written, and they altered the course of his life dramatically. He set sail on the Beagle on 27 December 1831.

When Darwin reached the tropics, three months later, and landed at Bahia in Brazil, he was totally thrilled and absorbed by the jungle; teeming with life. He also noticed straight away how dangerous the jungle was, with animals fighting to survive all the time. He collected thousands of specimens on the coast, and on his journeys inland. He started to collect fossils, found South of Buenos Aires. Darwin realised that these bones were very old, and belonged to animals no longer seen. He started to wonder about the idea of the whole world being created at the same time. He began to doubt that the earth, and all the living things on it, had been formed at one time.

He landed in the Galapagos Islands in 1835, and was fascinated by the different plants and animals on each small island. This was the place where his ideas really started to form; giving him real-life examples of animals superbly adapted to their environment, and found nowhere else on earth. He noticed the finches first, and their different beaks, as shown in the diagram below. He observed that on every small island, each species of finch had a different shaped beak, to allow it to feed on different foods, and so not compete with its neighbours. He made the same type of observation about the Giant Tortoises, which were so large they could hardly be missed, and again were adapted to feed on vegetation of different heights. He made many notes and scientific observations in his journal, collecting a vast amount of biological data on variation between organisms.

His ideas moved further forward when he worked with pigeons, selectively breeding them for particular characteristics. He was also helped by the work of Malthus, who wrote about the reproductive potential of man. Darwin applied this idea to other organisms, noting that despite producing large numbers of offspring, most populations

Type of finch	Beak shape	Food source	Habitat	Number of species
large ground finch (ancestral)	typical main land type: short and straight	crushing seed	coastal	1
ground finches	various, but short and straight as above	seeds/insects	coast/lowlands	3
cactus ground finches	long slightly curved, split-tongue	nectar of prickly-pear cactus	lowland	2
insectiverous tree finches	parrot-like	seeds/insects	forest	3
vegetarian tree finch	curved, parrot-like	fruit/buds/soft fruit	forest	1
warbler finch	slender	insects in flight	forest	1
woodpecker finch	large, straight, (uses cactus spine or stick to poke insects out of holes in wood)	larvae insect	forest	2

remained fairly constant. From this came his theory that there is intense competition to survive between the individuals in a population. Variations between individuals would mean that some were better adapted to survive in their environment than others. This would give organisms with favourable variations an advantage, and these would be more likely to survive, breed and pass on their characteristics to their offspring. Conversely, unfavourable characteristics as determined by the environment would be disadvantageous, and these organisms would be less likely to survive to breed.

At the same time that Darwin was coming to these conclusions, Alfred Wallace had also formulated the same ideas. Wallace sent Darwin an essay outlining his theories. This stimulated Darwin to agree to a joint presentation to the Linnean Society. A year later in 1859 he published the *Origin of Species*, explaining in it his ideas about evolution. His book sold out on the first day, and caused an outcry. The establishment was shocked that the idea of creation was being challenged. Darwin himself never got involved in the discussions and debates which followed. Its impact has changed human thinking to a greater extent than any book, other than the Bible.

The basic theory put forward by Darwin and Wallace can be outlined as follows:

- Individuals in a population have a greater reproductive capacity than the environment can sustain.
- There is therefore a *struggle for existence* within a population.
- In addition there is variation between individuals in any population.
- Some individuals are better adapted to their environment, giving them a *reproductive advantage*, and leading to *survival of the fittest*.
- These ideas collectively are called *evolution by natural selection*.

This work of Darwin and Wallace has been the basis of further study and the collection of more evidence in support of the theory, for generations of biologists. The theory has been extended and developed through evidence in many fields, some of which are outlined below. This is known as neo-Darwinism and is defined as *the theory of organic evolution by the natural selection of genetically determined characteristics*.

Palaeontology, the study of fossils, supports the idea of organisms changing over time; it also supports the concept that organisms have become more complex over time. One example where there is a near complete fossil record, documenting progressive changes in teeth and legs, is that of the horse. The record shows the evolution of the horse to the modern day, and the geographical distribution of the horse.

Another field of study providing evolutionary evidence is geographical distribution. This is often illustrated by the distribution of the camel family, which probably originated in North America. There are now several species in this family in different continents e.g. llamas in South America, camels in Africa. It is based on the idea that a species begins in one area, and spreads out from that place. As it does so the organisms adapt to the new environments they encounter. As a result of survival of the fittest, those best adapted reproduce and thrive. Their offspring change over time, to the point where they are so different from the original species, that even if they were to meet again they would be unable to breed. Hence a new species has been formed. In order for this to be true, there must be isolation of one group from the other, often by geographical features, such as mountains, rivers, deserts and oceans.

Comparative anatomy involves studying the anatomy of groups of animals, such as vertebrates. A good example of an organ, which has the same basic structure throughout the group, is seen in the pentadactyl limb of amphibia, reptiles, birds and mammals. This limb is based on five digits: fingers, toes, hence its name. As can be seen in the diagram below, the limb structure in all these types of animals is similar, and has a similar embryonic development. For this reason these are called homologous structures, because they have the same basic structure, demonstrating evolutionary links; this is even though their outward appearance is different, having adapted for use in walking, running, swimming or flying.

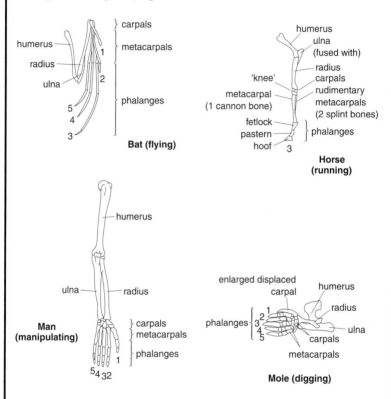

Comparative embryology shows similarity in stages of development in groups such as vertebrates, suggesting a common ancestry and supporting evolution.

Comparative biochemistry is one of the newest fields, providing evidence of links between groups through common types of chemicals. It can be seen that proteins have very similar or identical structures in closely related groups. For example the blood protein, haemoglobin, in humans and chimpanzees is almost identical.

After his momentous work on evolution, which included a second publication *The Descent of Man* in which he proposed that man and apes were descended from a common ancestor, Darwin led a quiet life in

Kent. He wrote other books about plants, orchids and worms. He was very famous by now, but he stayed out of public life. He became very ill in 1882, with sickness and fainting fits. Darwin died in his sleep on 19 April 1882. His wife and children wanted to bury him at home in Downe, but he was so famous by then that he was buried in Westminster Abbey.

Help desk

The essay on Darwin is about the complex and technical aspects of his work, and explores the effects and sense of outrage his theories caused. This means that the topic is dealt with in a complex way, as required at level 3. The other criteria for writing are also met e.g. writing complex sentences, using technical language. Spelling, punctuation and grammar is used at level 3.

Compare this to the straightforward way in which this topic is dealt with in the level 2 example, in Chapter 9.

Help desk

Images must be used to make a point or explain something. They must be an integral part of the document as a whole, and make it easier to understand. If the document would make less sense without the images, then they are being used correctly.

The example report on global warming has a diagram, which gives further explanation of the way in which greenhouse gases may cause a rise in temperature. It makes the idea, and the possible processes involved, easier to understand and is therefore integral to the document.

In the essay on Darwin, the images of the Galapagos finches illustrate the observations which formed a major part of Darwin's thinking. The diagrams of vertebrate limbs illustrate the ideas behind comparative anatomy. In both cases these points are integral to the text written, and they expand and explain complex points.

DEFINITIONS ▶

Extended document means at least three pages long. One of your pieces of writing will need to be an extended document at level 3. This means about three pages of text. It is likely to be a report, an essay, coursework or an assignment. This extended document must be the one which contains an image. In the examples in this chapter, the only three-page document is the essay. Since it has an image, it could be used as evidence of an extended document.

There is no need to over-do the length of your Communication written evidence, though. Remember that your work will be assessed for accuracy of spelling, grammar and punctuation. Although a few errors would be allowed in a long document, it is easier to maintain accuracy in a three-page document than in a 30-page one.

Organise your work coherently, using a suitable style:
- Use paragraphs.
- Indent the first line.
- Headings.
- Sub-headings.
- Highlight words, phrases or headings, using bold, italic, underlining, or colour.
- Link your ideas and arguments in complex sentences, using words like 'however' or 'therefore'.
- Treat the subject sensitively.
- Choose the appropriate layout and form for your purpose.
- Use a suitable style, such as a technical report, a set of instructions, descriptive writing, or a personal letter which expresses your feelings.
- The style must suit your purpose.

Help desk

Paragraphs are groups of sentences about the same subject or idea.

Show new paragraphs by indenting the first line, or leave a line between paragraphs.

Proofread your work and re-draft, to make sure that you have:

Spelt all words correctly by:

- Using a dictionary.
- Using a spell-checker (remember it does not check for meaning).
- Checking all unusual or technical words.
- At this level you should be able to spell everyday words without looking them up, and know how to check all unusual and technical words.

Using a dictionary:

- Words are listed in dictionaries in alphabetical order.
- The word is shown in bold.
- There is a letter, which tells you what type of word it is.
- There are explanations of the word's meaning(s).
- There are also abbreviations, and examples of use of the word, followed by the origin of the word.

Help desk

friend

Type of word = n = noun
Meanings = 1. a person well known to another and regarded with liking, affection, and loyalty; an intimate. 2. an acquaintance or associate. 3. an ally in a fight or cause; supporter....
Uses = 6. be friends (with). 7. make friends (with)
Origin = Old English *freond*...

Follow the rules of grammar, and make sure:

- The verb agrees with the subject.
- The tense is used consistently.
- The conditional form is properly used, e.g. 'if he comes, then I will not'.
- You can use the passive person e.g. 'it was done', rather than 'he did' or 'they did.' This type of writing is often used in scientific or technical reports.
- The sentence is divided up using commas.
- You can use link words such as 'however' and 'therefore'.

Examples:

She was very pleased with the gift, however she would have preferred the convertible sports model.

We were keen to get to the game on time, therefore we had to leave early, because we knew that the traffic would be very heavy.

Use correct punctuation:

- Punctuation is used to put a pause or space between words.
- This helps to make more sense of the words and to give emphasis, when speaking or reading.
- You should be able to use colons, semicolons, apostrophes and bullet points.
- Colons or dashes divide up sentences, or say the same thing but more clearly. They can also be used at the start of a list.
- Semicolons are pauses, which are longer than commas but shorter than full stops, to separate parts of a sentence.
- Apostrophes show belonging to, or the place where letters are missing in words.

Help desk

Remember it's = it is, with the apostrophe for the missing 'i'. Its has no apostrophe because it is like his or hers, when something belongs to it.

Examples:

Jane's Jaguar is very fast, but James' tractor goes anywhere.

The dog has had its day, but the cat is waiting for hers.

He didn't want to stop and say goodbye, because his train was leaving.

He's the one with all the money.

'Don't do that,' she said, 'because you may fall into the water'.

Help desk

Type of word:	How it is used:
Verb	A verb is used to describe an action.
	Examples: to run, to play, to hide, to laugh, to fight, to talk, to write.
	Verbs change depending on the tense, which tells you if the action happened in the past, is happening now, or will happen in the future.
	The form of the verb must agree with the subject.
	Examples: She did play with the dog. We fed the cat.
Noun	A noun is the name of a person, a place, an animal, plant or a thing.
	Examples: Peter, Peterborough, panther, primrose, pencil.
	The names of people, places, plants and animals are given capital letters.
Adjective	An adjective describes a noun or a pronoun.
	Examples: large, small, bad.
Adverb	An adverb describes a verb, or an adjective.
	Examples: quickly, sadly, good, badly.
Pronoun	A pronoun is used instead of a noun.
	Examples: she, he, it.

Help desk

Tense:

The tense tells you if the action happened in the past, is happening now, or will happen in the future. These are the past, present and future tenses.

In summary: Some Do's and Don'ts:

DO'S ✓

Use a suitable style of writing.
Follow the rules for different types of writing.
Plan and structure reports and essays.
Use pictures, charts and diagrams to make your points more clearly.
Proofread and re-draft.

DON'TS ✗

Wander away from the point or the question.
Spell words wrongly.
Use wrong punctuation.
Ignore the rules of grammar.

14

Communication Level 3: Practice Test Questions Based Mainly on Part A

Introduction

Now that you have developed and practised the Communication Skills set out in Part A of the unit, you are ready to try some short answer and multiple choice questions. If you find any of the questions difficult go back to Chapter 9 for more help before moving on with the book.

Here are some short answer and longer questions to check that you have all the skills and knowledge as set out in Part A. These are followed by example questions, illustrating the type of questions in the external tests. The external test will not have questions on discussions or spoken presentations.

Short answer questions

Discussions: Speaking and Listening

ACTIVITY

Prepare for and take part in a discussion about gender inequality in a developed country such as Britain, compared with a developing country such as Afghanistan.

Carry out some research, make notes, and be prepared to contribute to the discussion. This is a sensitive issue, so remember to consider the feelings of others.

1. You could decide to research a particular aspect of gender roles, such as the employment situation, education opportunities, or the religious or cultural aspects of gender. Try to divide up the topic into different areas, so that different people have specific areas to contribute to the debate. You could research the situation in several different countries between you.

2. Take part in the discussion. Try to contribute sensitively; accept the views and feelings of others, even though they are different from your own. Develop your own

points and encourage others to expand on their position so that everyone understands what is meant, and how people feel about the issues.

3. Now fill in the self evaluation about the discussion below. Try to be as honest as possible. Use your evaluation to improve on future discussions, such as those suggested in parts two and three of this book.

Self Evaluation:

When I spoke I made the following points:

I listened to these people speak:

I answered these questions:

Did you interrupt anyone?   Yes ☐   No ☐

I asked these questions:

Something I liked about the discussion:

Something I need feedback on:

Something which I would change in my next discussion is:

Ask one of the other people in the discussion or an observer to complete this audience evaluation, to support your own views above:

Observer or Peer Evaluation:

Something which I liked about the way ....took part in the discussion is:

Something which .... did very well in the discussion is:

Something which .... could have done better in the discussion is:

Presentation

ACTIVITY

Make notes for a presentation on a piece of AS/A level coursework or an investigation, or a GNVQ/CVE assignment, to be given to the rest of your group:

1. Plan your presentation, make notes, organise them. Choose suitable images, to explain some of your points, such as a chart, diagram or graph of your results or findings.

2. Make your presentation to a group of people.

3. Now fill in the self evaluation about the presentation below. Try to be as honest as possible. Use it to improve on future presentations which you give, such as those suggested in parts two and three of this book.

Self Evaluation:

I was pleased with this part of my presentation:

I was unsure about this part of my presentation:

I need feedback on this aspect of my presentation:

I could improve on:

Structure

Speaking skills

Tone

Gestures

Use of visual aids/images

I will try to improve my next presentation in the following way(s):

Ask one of the people in the audience to complete this audience evaluation, to support your own views above.

Observer or Peer Evaluation:

Something which I liked about the presentation is:

Something which .... did very well in the presentation is:

Something which .... could have done better in the presentation is:

Reading and Synthesising

ACTIVITY

Use the data in the table overleaf, from a holiday brochure, to answer the following questions:

a) Which country/city has temperatures consistently above 90°F throughout the year?

b) Which cities have August temperatures above 92°F and at least 12 hours of sunshine?

c) Which cities have less than 2mm rainfall and more than 10 hours of sunshine through June to September?

Turn to page 194 for answers.

	JAN			FEB			MARCH			APRIL			MAY			JUNE			JULY			AUG			SEP			OCT			NOV			DEC		
	Far.	Sun	Rain	Far.	Sun	Rain	Far.	Sun	Rain	Far.	Sun	Rain	Far.	Sun	Rain	Far.	Sun	Rain	Far.	Sun	Rain	Far.	Sun	Rain	Far.	Sun	Rain	Far.	Sun	Rain	Far.	Sun	Rain	Far.	Sun	Rain
INDIAN SUBCONTINENT																																				
INDIA Agra	73	9	0	78	9	0	89	10	0	101	10	0	107	10	1	105	8	2	94	6	8	91	6	10	93	8	5	92	10	1	85	10	0	76	8	0
Cochin	89	8	1	90	8	1	91	8	1	92	7	4	90	8	13	85	4	27	84	6	30	84	6	16	85	7	12	87	6	11	88	9	6	89	8	2
Delhi	70	8	1	75	9	1	87	8	1	97	9	0	105	9	1	102	7	3	96	6	7	93	6	7	93	8	4	93	9	1	84	9	0	73	7	0
Goa	88	8	0	90	9	0	90	10	0	91	9	1	88	9	2	88	4	23	84	4	31	84	3	14	84	5	11	88	7	5	91	8	1	91	9	0
MALDIVES Malé	85	6	2	85	7	0	86	8	0	87	8	2	86	7	7	85	5	12	84	6	10	84	6	14	83	6	9	80	5	5	74	5	10	67	5	3
NEPAL Kathmandu	61	6	1	67	6	2	77	8	3	83	10	2	86	7	10	85	5	10	84	3	15	83	4	14	83	6	6	74	5	1	65	6	0
SRI LANKA Colombo	86	8	3	87	9	3	88	8	6	88	7	9	87	6	15	85	5	9	85	6	5	85	6	4	85	6	6	85	7	14	85	6	12	85	8	6
FAR EAST & PACIFIC																																				
AUSTRALIA Sydney	79	7	4	79	7	3	77	6	6	72	6	5	67	6	5	63	5	4	62	6	6	64	6	2	68	7	3	72	7	3	74	7	3	77	7	4
BURMA (Myanmar) Rangoon	90	8	0	91	9	0	97	8	0	97	10	2	91	7	12	86	4	19	84	3	23	84	3	21	86	5	16	88	6	7	88	7	3	88	7	0
CHINA Canton (Guangzhou)	63	4	3	63	3	3	69	3	6	77	3	6	85	5	10	85	5	10	88	7	8	88	6	9	85	6	5	83	6	2	74	6	1	69	5	1
Peking (Beijing)	34	7	0	39	7	1	52	7	1	70	7	1	80	9	2	85	7	7	86	5	11	84	7	8	79	8	2	68	7	1	48	6	0	37	6	0
FIJI Suva	86	5	11	86	6	11	86	6	14	84	5	12	81	6	9	80	5	7	79	5	7	79	6	8	79	5	8	81	6	10	83	7	10	85	6	12
HONG KONG Hong Kong	64	5	1	63	3	3	67	3	5	75	4	7	82	6	11	85	5	15	87	8	17	87	7	15	85	7	11	81	7	7	74	6	6	68	6	4
INDONESIA Bali	88	8	9	88	8	8	88	10	8	88	10	5	88	9	4	87	9	2	87	9	1	87	10	0	88	11	1	90	10	1	90	9	6	88	9	9
JAPAN Tokyo	47	6	3	48	6	6	54	5	10	63	6	10	71	6	9	76	5	12	83	6	9	86	7	6	79	4	9	69	6	11	60	6	6	52	6	2
MALAYSIA Borneo	86	6	10	88	8	8	88	8	8	88	9	8	89	9	6	91	7	5	86	6	6	87	6	9	87	7	9	87	6	11	86	6	12	87	5	11
Kuala Lumpur	90	6	6	92	7	8	92	10	8	91	11	9	90	5	7	90	6	5	89	7	6	90	6	7	88	4	9	86	5	14	86	5	10	88	5	11
Kuantan	92	6	11	85	7	6	88	8	6	89	11	6	90	9	5	88	9	4	89	7	5	89	7	6	88	5	7	89	7	16	86	5	24	83	5	22
Langkawi	90	8	1	92	8	0	91	8	6	90	9	7	89	6	11	88	5	13	87	7	8	87	5	12	86	4	16	86	5	17	88	7	8	87	7	8
Penang	92	8	3	92	9	1	92	8	8	91	9	11	90	6	11	90	7	8	87	7	7	86	7	10	88	5	14	89	5	17	88	6	12	87	7	8
NEW ZEALAND Auckland	75	7	7	73	7	5	72	6	6	69	5	8	63	4	11	59	4	13	57	4	14	60	5	12	60	5	11	65	6	10	66	7	8	70	7	7
SINGAPORE Singapore	86	5	10	88	6	7	88	7	9	88	7	11	89	6	11	88	6	7	88	6	6	87	5	8	88	5	9	87	5	12	87	5	10	87	4	10
TAHITI Papeete	89	6	10	91	6	10	89	9	7	97	8	6	87	7	4	86	7	3	86	8	2	90	8	2	89	7	3	88	7	5	88	7	6	87	6	9
THAILAND Bangkok	84	9	1	86	9	1	90	8	1	95	9	2	93	8	6	91	6	6	89	5	6	88	5	7	88	5	12	88	6	8	87	8	3	87	8	1
Chiang Mai	87	9	1	91	9	1	97	9	1	97	8	2	93	8	5	90	6	6	89	4	6	88	4	7	89	5	11	88	6	5	87	7	3	82	9	1
Hua Hin	89	*	1	89	*	0	93	*	1	95	*	1	93	*	5	93	*	5	89	*	4	90	*	4	89	*	5	88	*	6	86	*	7	87	*	3
Koh Samui	89	3	2	91	9	1	95	9	1	95	8	2	93	6	5	91	6	6	90	6	3	90	5	4	89	4	5	86	6	11	85	8	14	84	9	7
Pattaya	89	9	1	90	9	1	91	9	2	95	9	2	88	10	6	88	6	5	88	6	4	88	6	4	86	5	10	85	6	12	87	8	3	84	9	3
Phuket/Krabi	89	9	1	91	9	1	91	9	2	91	9	2	88	8	12	88	6	13	88	5	10	87	5	10	86	5	13	87	6	12	87	8	8	87	9	3
Rayong	89	9	1	90	9	1	95	9	2	95	8	2	93	8	10	91	6	10	90	5	10	90	5	10	89	5	10	88	6	10	87	8	3	87	9	1
VIETNAM Saigon/Ho Chi Minh	93	5	1	95	6	0	97	5	1	98	5	2	96	4	9	93	3	13	91	4	12	92	4	11	92	5	13	91	4	11	91	4	4	91	4	2
MIDDLE EAST																																				
DUBAI Dubai	76	8	0	77	8	1	82	8	1	90	10	0	99	12	0	102	12	0	105	11	0	104	11	0	102	10	0	95	10	0	87	10	0	80	9	0
EGYPT Aswan	75	7	0	79	8	0	87	8	0	96	9	0	103	10	0	107	10	0	107	11	0	107	11	0	104	10	0	98	8	0	88	9	0	78	7	0
Cairo	65	9	0	69	8	0	75	9	0	83	10	0	91	11	0	95	12	0	96	12	0	95	12	0	90	11	0	86	10	0	78	9	0	68	8	0
Hurghada	60	9	0	62	10	0	65	10	0	75	11	0	80	12	0	87	13	0	89	13	0	90	12	0	86	11	0	82	10	0	73	9	0	68	8	0
Sharm El Sheikh	73	8	0	77	10	0	77	11	0	77	11	0	102	12	0	90	12	0	91	12	0	92	12	0	86	11	0	84	10	0	75	9	0	70	8	0
Luxor	62	9	0	69	10	0	84	10	1	95	11	0	102	12	0	106	12	0	105	12	0	105	12	0	101	11	0	95	10	0	76	9	1	76	6	2
JORDAN Amman	54	7	3	56	7	3	60	8	4	73	10	1	81	11	1	87	13	0	90	13	0	90	13	0	88	11	0	81	10	0	72	8	0	59	6	6
LEBANON Beirut	62	7	7	63	5	5	66	6	4	72	7	2	76	11	1	80	12	0	85	12	0	86	12	0	84	11	1	80	10	2	73	9	4	65	6	6
OMAN Muscat	77	9	1	77	9	0	82	9	0	90	10	0	97	11	0	99	11	1	95	10	0	91	10	0	93	10	0	91	11	0	86	9	0	79	9	1

ACTIVITY

Synthesise the main points from the following piece of writing about a mobile phone. The important information concerns two main areas, but is not very easy to pick out in its present format:

1. Care and maintenance of the phone.

2. Safety information when using the phone.

Using the two headings convert the following information into two lists as a set of bullet points under each heading. Make the points concise, and written as a set of instructions. Insert an image as part of your lists:

Ernitron Mobile Phone

Congratulations on purchasing your Ernitron mobile phone, which you will find to be a product of superior design. Your new phone is well crafted using the very latest in hi-tech materials, and should be treated with care. Keep your phone dry, free from dust and avoid leaving it in very cold, or very hot places. You should also avoid the use of chemicals such as solvents or detergents for cleaning. The phone should not be dropped or shaken.

To get the best from your phone, you will want to use it safely, and with the best possible reception. Reception can be improved by moving around within a room, or standing near the window. Sometimes you may have to go outside.

You should not use your hand-held phone while driving, always park your vehicle first. Avoid interference with other electronic devices such as pacemakers, by ensuring a distance of at least 20 cm (6') between the phone and the pacemaker. The phone should not be carried in a breast pocket, and should be switched off immediately if you suspect any interference.

Some mobile phones may interfere with hearing aids, or other medical equipment, contact our customer service line for more information (088888 123456). Switch off your phone in hospitals and health care facilities. Rarely your phone could affect electronic systems in your motor vehicle, such as air bag systems or anti-lock braking systems. Consult the vehicle manufacturer.

Do not use your phone in a potentially explosive atmosphere, such as at service stations, below deck on boats, grain storage facilities, or chemical storage facilities. Finally do not attempt to open or repair your phone. Qualified personnel only should service or repair the phone, or install it in a vehicle.

Turn to page 195 for the suggested lists of instructions.

ACTIVITY

Pick out the main points from the following article about outward-bound centres:

The culture secretary, Chris Smith, will today unveil a £50m scheme to create outward bound centres to enable city teenagers to experience the challenges of outdoor adventure. Mr Smith will tell Labour's conference that the need to provide such opportunities to 16 and 17-year olds has emerged from the government's research into social exclusion.

Youngsters likely to drop out of school early would be better off spending their last months in such schemes rather than 'sitting around making mayhem in school', ministers have concluded.

But the plan's underlying inspiration dates from the walks Mr Smith used to take across Scotland's mountains with his namesake, the late Labour leader, John Smith, who set out to tackle all 284 peaks known as the Munros.

The dozens of outward bound centres, expected to be created from the national lottery's new opportunities fund, may be called 'John Smith centres' in honour of the highlander who led Labour from 1992 to his sudden death in 1994 when Tony Blair succeeded him. 'He would have longed to see us giving children the opportunity to reach out beyond the concrete confines of the towns and cities,' Chris Smith will say.

Turn to page 195 for a list of the main points.

Writing

ACTIVITY

Make notes for a presentation about living a healthy lifestyle. Find an image to make one of your points.

Write a report about your intended career. Include information about entry, training or HE requirements; salary; career progression opportunities; a day in the life of; personal characteristics needed. Has your perception of the career changed following your research?

Short and longer answer questions on pages 191–194

Holiday brochure answers:

a) Vietnam, Saigin/Ho Chi Minh

b) Cairo, Luxor

c) Cairo, Hurghada, Sharm El Sheikh, Luxor, Amman

Ernitron Phone instructions:

Care and maintenance list	Safety information
• Keep phone dry and dust free.	• For improved reception move to a window or go outside.
• Do not store in very hot/very cold conditions.	• Do not use your phone while driving.
• Do not use cleaning solvent or detergents.	• If you wear a pacemaker, keep the phone at least 20 cm away from it, do not carry the phone in your breast pocket.
• Do not shake or drop the phone.	
• Do not attempt to repair your phone, use qualified person.	• Switch off phone in hospitals, service stations, chemical or grain storage facilities, inside boats (phone customer service for more information on 088888 123456).

Suitable images could include the phone crossed through in various situations, such as driving, at a petrol station, or in a hospital.

New Outward Bound centres

Main points:
- The Government is to spend £50 million of lottery money to create dozens of outward bound centres for 16-17 year olds from inner cities.
- The places will be for youngsters at the end of school career, rather than have them drop out.
- The inspiration for the plan is the late Labour leader, John Smith, who was a keen highland walker.

Test questions (external assessment)

Now try these short and longer answer questions, which will test your Communication skills in the same way as the one and a half hour external assessment. Dictionaries are not allowed in the test. You will have 90 minutes to answer all the questions, which give a total of 50 marks. The paper will be divided into two parts:

1) Part A short answer questions, which you should allow 45 minutes to complete. There are 25 marks allocated to this part.

2) Part B extended answer question, which you should allow 45 minutes to complete. There are 25 marks allocated to this part, including 9 marks for spelling, punctuation and grammar.

There will be source materials to read, and use to answer the questions. Usually there are two or three documents about the same subject, but with different views or perspectives. You are then asked to answer questions, which will test your skills in the areas of:

- Reading information.
- Summarising information.
- Synthesising information.
- Understanding meanings of text and images (comprehension).
- Identifying opinion and bias.
- Identifying relevant information.
- Writing in different styles.
- Writing using different formats for documents.
- Writing using correct spelling, punctuation and grammar.
- The three documents are usually three sides of A4 in total, ie an extended document.

The answers to the following example questions can be found on page 205. Try to answer the questions yourself, before you check them. Remember that dictionaries are not allowed in the test. The test paper booklet provides spaces in which to answer the questions. This gives you some idea of how much you should write.

Using the information in Articles 1, 2, 3, provided, answer the short questions below:

1. What do each of the three images and headlines, reporting on the fuel shortage, portray?

   (7 marks)

Article 1

SHOWDOWN AT THE PUMPS

By David Smith

Government could call in troops to help break the blockade of refineries

FUEL protestors were last night poised for a major confrontation with the Government after it emerged that troops could be called in to help thousands of police end the national blockade of depots and refineries.

Panic buying reached new highs with car queues of more than a mile to some filling stations and several frantic drivers brawling to get to the pumps. One motorist, 62-year-old Anthony Probert, died yesterday in a queue for petrol at a Safeway filling station in Abergavenny, Gwent. He is thought to have suffered a heart attack in the soaring heat. Elsewhere, some garages exploited the queues, with independent owner Paul Gizzonio in Derby causing outrage by hiking up prices to more than £11 a gallon (£2.50 a litre). More than 200 filling stations in the North-west ran dry, but growing fears saw long queues drain the pumps in other regions, including London. Some motorway service stations also dried up and a number of ambulance and fire services began restricting non-emergency work to conserve dwindling stocks.

Last night a North Wales hospital group cancelled all non-emergency operations as a precaution. Kent Fire Brigade decided to answer only 999 calls, Leicester police ordered its officers to use patrol cars for only essential journeys, and the West Yorkshire ambulance service cancelled all non-emergency journeys to and from hospitals across the region.

Cotswold District Council officials said they only had enough fuel to keep collecting rubbish until tomorrow, while Cheltenham Borough Council suspended its service at a waste tip to cut back on the cost of wagons transporting bulky rubbish.

As the Prime Minister declared he would never give in to the protestors, the Privy Council was sanctioning the use, if necessary, of powers to require oil companies to ensure the distribution of fuel across the country.

Armed with the emergency powers, the Cabinet's civil

contingencies committee chaired by the Home Secretary Jack Straw met later in the day to discuss whether the police needed help from the Army to break up the blockades.

Despite the widespread disruption to ordinary motorists, most expressed sympathy with the protestors. Daniel Cooper, 27, a graphic designer from Wolverhampton, who was caught up in a traffic jam caused by a blockade, said: 'I was stuck for over two hours and for a lot of the time I was stationary.

'But I'd expected this to happen so I wasn't put out by it all. In fact I think most people support this protest.' Tony Blair, however, said there was no question of a Government climbdown. On a two-day tour of northern England, he said: 'We cannot and will not alter Government policy on petrol through blockades and pickets.

'That is not the way we make policy in Britain and, as far as I'm concerned, it never will be.'

Mr Blair said the only 'sensible' way Britain could lower fuel prices was by putting pressure on Opec, the organisation of oil producing companies, and not to bow to pressure from blockades.

Yesterday Mr Blair saw forecourt-chaos first hand from his chauffeur-driven Jaguar in Leicestershire as he drove past fuming motorists queueing for fuel.

And last night protestors banged on the bonnet of his Jaguar as he left Hull City Hall and a handful of people shouted: 'Shame on you! Shame on you!' Mounted police cantered along the road to clear the way for the car.

More protestors surrounded a restaurant where Mr Blair and his deputy John Prescott were to have met party workers.

They succeeded in preventing Mr Blair going there and Mr Prescott was 90 minutes late arriving with his wife Pauline.

A spokesman said: 'The Prime Minister is sad that the protest has led to this type of destruction and disappointment for the hundreds of party members who were due to attend this dinner with John Prescott. The whole Government has sent out a strong signal to the police that they have every support, the full backing of the Prime Minister and other Ministers to keep fuel supplies moving. The public can be assured their supplies of fuel will be moving and panic buying is unnecessary.'

Earlier, Number 10 had dismissed the mounting petrol crisis as a collection of 'isolated problems' despite the crisis threatening to engulf the entire country by the end of the week.

Tory frontbencher Nigel Evans said the Number 10 reaction was like Jim Callaghan's 1979 blunder about the country's strike-bound Winter of Discontent - 'Crisis, what crisis?'

Article 1 continued

From couriers to clowns, thousands are being driven round the bend

By Simon Bird and Mark Blacklock

THE fuel crisis is already having a devastating effect on thousands of people, from driving schools and zoo keepers to travelling showmen and hotels.

Bullocks Coachways, of Cheadle, Cheshire, is running low on fuel and may have to axe some routes. Director Geoff Bullock and his staff spent yesterday searching for supplies with the firm's fuel storage tanks containing enough for only the next two days.

'We are in talks with transport chiefs to see which routes we can legally suspend,' said Mr Bullock.

The clowns weren't smiling when the Great British Circus pitched its big top at Newcastle upon Tyne. Suppliers who usually guarantee a weekly 1,500-litre diesel delivery can't say when they will be able to make another.

The 40 show people could not practise or rehearse, or even watch television while relaxing, because generators were being saved for use only during a performance.

Worried holidaymakers are cancelling trips to such popular home destinations as the Lake District. At Windermere Jim Casey said four guests from Birmingham and two from London had cancelled bookings at his Beaumont Hotel over the weekend.

Keepers at the Welsh Mountain Zoo in Colwyn Bay are worried about fuel blockades halting food deliveries for the animals. Zoo director Chris Jackson said: 'We don't grow our own food here and we need fresh fruit, vegetables and meat.'

Yesterday's unluckiest motorist was a man who queued for 90 minutes at a coastal filling station in North Wales – only to find when he reached the pump that he couldn't get his petrol cap off. He drove away.

Article 2

I'M ALL RIGHT JAG

Blair snubs fuel campaign .. but it doesn't affect him, does it?

By Christian Fraser

TONY Blair glides past petrol-starved drivers in his Jaguar yesterday after vowing to smash the fuel blockade.

Mr Blair was all right – he will always have a full tank. But Britain was in crisis as more than 1,000 filling stations ran dry and prices soared as high as £11.36 a gallon. Pledging not to bow to protestors' demands to cut fuel taxes, Mr Blair said last night he would give 'strong support' to whatever police had to do.

Earlier, he declared in Loughborough, Leics: 'We cannot, and will not, alter Government policy on petrol through blockades and pickets.

'That's not the way to make policy in Britain and, as far as I'm concerned, it never will be.'

Late last night the Government confirmed that the Privy Council and the Queen had sanctioned the use, if necessary, of special contingency powers to make sure fuel was delivered.

A DTI spokeswoman said Energy Minister Helen Liddell had met the Queen at Balmoral to seek royal approval for the move.

Secretary of State for Industry Stephen Byers said: 'It is important that vital services are maintained.

'We will take whatever steps are needed to ensure that priority users, such as the health services, schools and public transport, are supplied with fuel.'

The President of the Association

of Chief Police Officers, Sir John Evans, said: 'We will be doing everything in our power to ensure that physical access to oil installations is kept open and that people who wilfully obstruct the access from such sites are dealt with firmly within the law.'

Earlier yesterday Mr Blair was at No. 10 for the first meeting of a Civil Contingency Committee, chaired by Home Secretary Jack Straw.

Together with Chancellor Gordon Brown and Mr Byers, they drew up a 'battle plan' in case the dispute begins to hit fuel supplies for emergency vehicles and hospitals.

A Government source said the meeting was a 'sensible and routine precaution' but added that ministers were not expecting a 'winter of discontent' and that the blockades would not last much longer.

The Home Office said last night: 'So far, police tactics have been low-key. That is going to change.'

Downing Street added: 'It is the Prime Minister's strong view that whatever people feel about the price of petrol – and he understands how they feel – he does not believe public sympathy is with this kind of protest.'

'Police have the full backing of the Prime Minister and other ministers to keep fuel supplies moving and panic buying is unnecessary.'

A spokeswoman denied reports that troops could be used to ensure supplies reached hospitals, schools and emergency services.

She added: 'There is no question of troops being deployed.'

'As far as we are concerned this is an operational matter for the police.'

During his visit to Leicestershire, Mr Blair and his official Jaguar were spotted passing a petrol station queue in Hathern.

The Premier was heading for Hull to mark Deputy Prime Minister John Prescott's 30 years as an MP in the city.

After a ceremony at the City Hall, two protestors banged on the bonnet of Mr Blair's car.

Later, a blockade by lorries, tractors and taxis kept Mr Blair away from a celebration dinner date with his No. 2.

Fuel prices jumped more than 40 per cent from January 1999 to June this year. The Government blames recent rises on world oil prices.

Article 3

Privy Council gives Blair emergency powers but police say protests cannot be halted

Panic as oil blockade bites

Peter Hetherington, Jamie Wilson, Paul Kelso and Patrick Wintour

The Government yesterday sought emergency powers to quell the growing fuel crisis in the strongest demonstration yet that it will not cave in to the blockades that have all but crippled petrol distribution across large swathes of the country.

Following the public declaration by Tony Blair that he would not cave in to the most widespread picketing seen in Britain for 15 years, the government yesterday convened a rare meeting of an emergency Cabinet committee which considered whether troops should be deployed to aid the supply of fuel to essential services.

The crisis has now also drawn the Queen into the political drama after senior ministers travelled to Balmoral to hold a meeting with her of the privy council yesterday afternoon.

However, police officers said that many of the demonstrators blockading refineries were not breaking the law, and that some lorry drivers were refusing to deliver petrol in an act of solidarity with colleagues on the other side of the picket lines.

Assistant Chief Constable Meredydd Hughes of Greater Manchester Police said: 'Although we currently have a protest in Trafford Park there is currently no fuel blockade or picket. Suppliers and fuel contractors are free to move fuel if they choose to do so; however the situation is that tanker drivers are making the decision not to move supplies after discussions with protestors.'

With panic-buying closing hundreds of filling stations around Britain, rationing in force in many areas and emergency services restricting all but non-essential calls, Tony Blair hardened his line by calling on the Home Secretary, Jack Straw, to ensure that extra police will be available.

John Reid, the Scottish secretary, who is speaking for the government on the issue, said last night: 'Any action that is appropriate will be taken.'

Mr Reid urged the public to stay calm and said panic buying, not the blockade of refineries and distribution centres, was the prime cause of current shortages.

Tony Blair was forced last night to cancel a dinner in Hull in honour of John Prescott due to fuel protestors blocking all the routes to the restaurant while earlier in the city the Prime Minister's car was temporarily blocked by a separate demonstration by pro-fox hunting supporters.

With six out of nine of Britain's refineries disrupted, and more than a quarter of petrol stations running out of fuel, oil companies said the position was becoming critical – with the north-west of England, and South Wales particularly badly hit. No filling stations in Cardiff appear to be open.

While ministers rejected calls from leaders of petrol retailers for a reduction in fuel duty, oil companies privately made clear that the government, rather than the industry, should sort out the crisis because of the huge bonus the Treasury had received in North Sea taxation from the 10 year high in oil prices.

At the TUC in Glasgow, several union leaders urged the government to reduce fuel duty to make British industry more competitive.

With both Tony Blair and Chancellor Gordon Brown due at the TUC today, protestors – not the delegates – are preparing to give them a rowdy reception.

Article 3 continued

Farming militants behind the action

Peter Hetherington

A committee of 12 militant farmers is one of the driving forces behind the nationwide picketing refineries and fuel depots propelling Britain towards a fuel crisis.

Called Farmers for Action, it was launched at a service station on the M5 near Birmingham earlier this year amid growing disenchantment over the reluctance of the National Farmers' Union and the Country Landowners Association to confront ministers with tougher tactics in defence of the beleaguered industry.

Another, looser alliance in North Wales was partly responsible for the more spontaneous protest which launched the nationwide action at Stanlow oil refinery in Cheshire five days ago.

FFA says action took off following an informal meeting at Ruthin auction mart in North Wales a week ago. Hard-pressed farmers, who first launched French-style protests in Britain late in 1997 by tipping Irish beefburgers into Holyhead docks, called for blockades over rising fuel prices. They were joined by hauliers, whose own protests of slow-moving convoys earlier this year came to nothing and were ridiculed by ministers.

It is clear that the looser alliance of Welsh farmers also played a significant part. Led by Brynle Williams, from Cilcain, near Mold, and a farming neighbour, Clive Swann, they regard themselves as the vanguard of the militant farming army.

2. Summarise the main points being reported about the effects of the fuel shortage, in the three articles.

   (9 marks)

3. Compare the approach taken in the three articles, in terms of factual presentation, political opinion and bias.

   (9 marks)

Turn to page 205 for the answers.

4. Extended answer question.

   (25 marks)

You work for an MP and have been asked to write a report on the fuel crisis, giving your view on the way that ordinary people are being affected. You also need to express your assessment of the mood of the country regarding the cause of the crisis, and the public perception of the Government's handling of the crisis. Your report will be based on the information given in the articles.

In writing your report you should:

- Use an appropriate format and style.
- Use information from all the articles.
- Organise your material clearly and coherently using your own words.
- Present your own interpretation of what has been written by synthesising the information into a report.
- Write clearly, using accurate spelling, punctuation and grammar.

See below and pages 205 for the answers.

Short answer questions on pages 196–205

1. Image one headed 'Showdown at the pumps' portrays the pump as a weapon/gun. The headline conveys the idea of confrontation or battle over petrol prices/taxes.

   (2 marks)

   Image two headed 'I'm all right jag' portrays the Prime Minister, Tony Blair, as driving a large car/Jaguar, which uses a lot of fuel. It also shows his car cruising past other motorists, because he has fuel, while they have to queue for hours for petrol. An unsympathetic/arrogant politician, who does not care what is happening to the ordinary motorist.

   (3 marks)

   Image three shows that many petrol stations across the country have run out of fuel. The focus is on the panic as people try to get petrol, and on the Government's response to the crisis/the measures being taken to help.

   (2 marks)

2. Article one reports confrontation, panic buying, queues and brawls. It reports the death of one motorist in a queue. The article then gives specific personal examples of how people are being individually affected, in terms of financial cost, potential loss of jobs, and cutting of essential services. More unusual examples are cited, of the effects on a circus, some holidaymakers and a zoo, with a humorous example at the end.

   (2 marks)

Article two focuses on the Government's response, and refusal to bow to the pressure being created. It outlines the Government contingency committee meeting, and battle plans. The police response and intentions, and the effect on the Prime Minister's arrangements for a visit to Hull are covered. It also explains the effects of picketing of fuel depots and refineries, in individual towns and cities.

(2 marks)

Article three again focuses on the Government's intention not to give in, and the response and intentions of the police. It summarises the number of petrol stations without fuel, and emphasises the Government message to the public, not to panic buy, and so create the effect of a shortage. The effect on the Prime Minister's schedule is covered, with reports on the views of oil companies and trade unions, urging the Government to reduce fuel duty. There is a side article, suggesting that militant farmers have played a significant part in the blockades of oil refineries, supermarket distribution depots and dairies.

(2 marks)
(3 marks) for synthesis of key information, which is expressed in a suitable form.

3. Articles two and three focus on Government and police responses. Both cover the Privy Council meeting with the Queen, and the effect of the crisis on the Prime Minister's schedule. Article three goes on to suggest that panic buying, not the blockades, are the source of the fuel shortage. It also draws attention to the role of militant farmers in the crisis.

(2 marks)

Article one, in comparison, is much more personal in its reporting and draws attention to the effects of the crisis on individuals, such as loss of earnings, and jobs. It mentions confrontations on an individual level in queues, thus drawing a parallel with the national level confrontation, between protestors and Government. It also reports on the unusual and extraordinary effects, such as the death of one motorist, and one who queued for hours and could not get the petrol cap off.

(2 marks)

Politically, article two is openly critical of the most senior member of the Government, and personalises its criticism. It also makes the effects of the crisis more real, by writing about the effects on individuals. The first article is all about confrontation between Government and protestors, on a more national level. Articles two and three, refer to the Government's response, and dealing with the situation. They both comment on the effects of the crisis on both individuals within the Government, and the Government as a whole.

(2 marks)
Synthesis of key information, which is expressed in a suitable form. (3 marks)

4. Extended question

Report on Fuel crisis of September 2000

Public perception of the crisis

- The current crisis is perceived by the parts of the public as being caused by high fuel prices, partly due to taxation. There is a mixed view within the public as to the cause of the crisis, some blaming the Government and others the protestors.

- There is some sympathy with road hauliers and farmers, because the effect of high fuel prices is damaging their business. There is also a perception that people living in areas without good public transport facilities have no choice but to use their cars, and so this is an additional burden of tax on many people.

Public perceptions of the Government and its actions

- Public transport is perceived as inadequate nationally. This inadequacy means that everyone is 'forced' to use their car sometimes, and that most people find car ownership essential. This in turn means people pay more tax, through fuel and vehicle duty.

- The fact that people have created the crisis themselves by panic buying is not a widely held view. The Government are presented as being ill-prepared for a crisis which they should have seen coming. In some quarters they are also seen as arrogant, and not prepared to listen to the electorate.

- Many people are prepared to put up with the inconvenience to themselves, but not to accept the potentially drastic effects on essential services, such as hospitals, schools, and emergency services. As time goes on they are likely to become much less tolerant of the personal inconvenience caused as well.

(25 marks) including marks for:

a) using an appropriate format, in this case a report, with headings, and formal language. (4 marks)

b) organising the information clearly in a structured way, presenting perceptions. (10 marks)

c) writing legibly, using accurate spelling, grammar and punctuation. (10 marks)

15

Communication Level 3: Activities for Practice (Part A) or Assessment (Part B)

Introduction

This part of the book will help you to practise all the skills set out in Part A of the Communication unit and check you have all the required knowledge. Once you are ready you can use these skills in assignments and tasks and in everyday situations in work, school or college, to produce evidence for your portfolio.

In this section you will also start to get ideas for assignments, which you can use as evidence in your portfolio. This is needed to meet Part B of the unit.

When you have practised your skills, you will be ready to plan activities and assignments, to apply your skills, and to show what you can do.

Use the following sheet to keep an on-going record of your developing skills and knowledge. Use it to record examples of tasks and assignments, which have helped you to practise your skills. Remember this is about practising your skills. You may only need one example here, or you may need more than two, depending upon your skill level when you start this unit.

Communication Part A	One example of an activity which has helped me develop and practise my skills is:	One example of an activity which has helped me develop and practise my skills is:
3.1a Discussions		
Research information		
Make notes		
Make useful points		
Invite others to speak		
Be sensitive to the views of others		
Listen carefully for tone, mood		
Watch gestures of others		
Use your own body language to show you are listening		
Ask questions		
3.1b Presentation		
Research topic		
Make notes		
Use image(s)		
Speak clearly		
Use standard English		
Structure the presentation, to put points in a sensible order		
Engage the audience using image(s), relevant examples, and by varying tone		
3.2 Reading and Synthesising		
Use different sources including extended documents (3 pages)		
Skim sources picking out main points		
Scan texts		
Read for detail		
Use references		
Identify bias and opinions		
Synthesise for a presentation, essay or report		
3.3 Writing		
Write:		
Letter		
Memo		
Notes		
Report		
Essay		
Application form		
Use images		

Structure work with:
Paragraphs
Headings
Sub-headings
Indentation
Highlighting

Choose suitable style e.g.
formal, technical, narrative

Proofread, and redraft

Use accurate:
Spelling
Grammar
Punctuation

3.1 Discussions and Presentation

You could use any example of a discussion and a presentation, but if you want to use the evidence in your portfolio, someone needs to observe you and record your skills as having met the criteria as shown below. You will need to be supervised for this to take place and for your assessor to confirm your skills. You could use a video or audio tape as part of your evidence. You can help this process by keeping your own records and reflections of the discussion using the tracking and recording sheets like those which follow on page 215. These sheets can be used to show how your skills are developing. They could also be part of your portfolio evidence, to help show that you can use your skills in different situations.

Examples of discussions you could take part in to practise and apply your skills. The issues and topics must be complex, or dealt with in a complex way at level 3:

- What is art (Group)?
- Getting help if worried about sexually transmitted diseases (Group).
- HE interview with an admissions tutor (One-to-one).
- An employment interview (One-to-one).
- The use of recombinant DNA technology is morally and ethically acceptable (Group).
- Instruct someone to make an article, play a game, or use a piece of apparatus or equipment (One-to-one).

- Cigarette smoking is morally and ethically unacceptable, in view of the effects on health, and the high health care costs resulting from smoking, and should be banned (Group).
- Language and the way it is used has a powerful effect on the political system of any culture (Group).

Example:

Acceptability of Smoking

Preparation for group discussion:

Read:
→ Health leaflets
→ Text books
→ Internet sites e.g. Government health statistics

Summarise:
→ Effects of smoking on health e.g. the smoker, those around them.
→ Data on incidence of diseases caused by smoking e.g. statistics on lung cancer, heart disease; comparison of smokers with non-smokers.
→ Data on costs of health care.
→ Acceptability of banning smoking e.g. civil liberties, enforceability, addictiveness of nicotine as a drug.

Synthesise:
→ Ideas on moral acceptability of smoking e.g. costs of health care, which could be used in other ways.
→ Ideas on ethical acceptability of smoking e.g. research into the effects of smoking using animals.
→ Acceptability of refusing health care to smokers.
→ Effects of banning smoking.

Make notes of:
→ Points you want make from the summary and synthesis lists above.
→ Issues related to decision making on sensitive issues such as this.
→ The wishes of the majority in a democracy.
→ Possible options and their merits.

Taking part in a group discussion:
→ Listen to what others are saying.
→ Look at each person as they speak.
→ Be sensitive in your responses.
→ Speak clearly to make your points.
→ Answer questions.
→ Ask questions.
→ Invite people to speak.
→ Make useful suggestions.

Here are some examples of presentations you could make to practise and apply your skills. The issues and topics must be complex, or dealt with in a complex way at level 3:

- The effect of increasing human populations on world food supplies.
- Nature versus nurture; heredity versus environment, as the basis for natural selection.
- A training or fitness programme for team sport players e.g. rugby, hockey.
- Presentation of sales and profits for any company/product over a 12-month period.
- Your findings from an investigation in the field, for biology, geography, geology, PE, psychology, or other suitable subject/area.
- It is morally and ethically acceptable to use biotechnology to manipulate human reproduction.
- The history of brewing.
- The business world is driven by the need for profit, and takes little account of ethical and environmental issues.
- Change is an inherent feature of language, resulting from social and cultural causes.

Example:

Sales and Profits for Maxi-Mountain bikes

Preparation for presentation:

Read:
→ Data on manufacturing costs
→ Data on marketing costs
→ Data on sales
→ Data on profits
→ Analysis of market share for mountain bikes
→ Company reports

Summarise:
→ Annual costs
→ Annual sales
→ Annual profits
→ Comparisons with previous years
→ Sales projections

Synthesise:
→ Factors affecting costs
→ Factors affecting sales
→ Fluctuations in profit
→ Reliability of the market and therefore projections

Plan the presentation:
→ Who is the audience to be?
→ Use suitable images to illustrate complex points or issues e.g. costs, sales, profits graphs, charts, diagrams.
→ Prepare notes and resources.
→ Put it together in a logical sequence.
→ Identify any strengths/weaknesses in your report/proposals.
→ Plan for questions.

Deliver the presentation:
→ Speak clearly.
→ State your points in a way that suits the audience and situation.
→ Make the structure easy to follow.
→ Use images effectively.
→ Engage your audience.
→ Take questions.

Take feedback on the presentation:
→ From the audience.
→ From your assessor/supervisor.
→ Carry out a self evaluation.

Communication Part B Tracking and Recording Sheets:

Tracking and Recording sheets

Communication Level 3 Part B	Evidence must show you can:
C3.1a Discussions Contribute to a group discussion about a complex subject.	• Make clear and relevant contributions in a way that suits your purpose and situation. • Listen and respond sensitively to others, and develop points and ideas. • Create opportunities for others to contribute when appropriate.

I took part in a discussion with:

Date of the discussion:

The discussion was about:

The purpose of the discussion was:

I spoke clearly to make these points: 1
2
3

I listened to these points: 1
2
3

I asked these questions: 1
2
3

I moved the discussion forward by making these points: 1
2
3

I created these opportunities for others to speak. 1
2
3

Tracking and Recording sheets

Communication Level 3 Part B	Evidence must show you can:

C3.1b Presentation

Make a presentation about a complex subject, using at least one image to illustrate complex points.

- Speak clearly and adapt your style of presentation to suit your purpose, audience and situation.
- Structure what you say so that the sequence of information and ideas may be easily followed.
- Use a range of techniques to engage the audience including effective use of images.

I gave a presentation about:
Date of the talk:

To people I know/don't know

The purpose of the presentation was:

I spoke clearly to the audience to make these points:

1
2
3

I structured my talk, to make these points:

1
2
3

I used these images to make points:

1 Image:

Point
2 Image:

Point

I used these techniques to engage the audience:

1
2
3

Your signature:

Summary: Some common problems and solutions:

Summary

Problem	Solution
Not enough preparation	Be very clear about the topic.
	Take enough time.
	Make good notes.
Speaking too much, gabbling or rushing	Practise what you want to say *before* the discussion/presentation.
	Do not interrupt.
Speaking too little	Decide on one or two points that you will make.
	Practise what you want to say *before* the discussion/presentation.
Speaking too softly or quietly	Practise your presentation, speaking it out loud to someone you know well.
Not listening to others	It's easy to think that you have heard what someone has said, rather than what they did say.
	Focus on the speaker.
	Make notes if you need to.
	Try not to listen to what you want to hear.
Ignoring the views of others	Do not get too excited or agitated by someone else's point of view.
	Remember – not everyone thinks the same as you.
	Try not to listen to what you want to hear.
	Do not attack people for their point of view, don't make it personal.
Being insensitive to the feelings of others	Consider other people's perspective and point of view.
	Think about their feelings and experiences.

If you are having lots of problems, return to step one in Chapter 15. Check your checklists, go to the Help Desks and ask for advice if you need to, *before* you go on to the next set of practice tasks and assignments.

3.2 Reading and Synthesising

You could use any example of materials to read and synthesise, but if you want to use the evidence in your portfolio, someone needs to record your skills as having met the criteria. You can help this process by keeping your own records and reflections of the discussion using the tracking and recording sheets like those which follow on page 220. These sheets can be used to show how your skills are developing. They could also be part of your portfolio evidence, to help show that you can use your skills in different situations.

Here are some examples of some topics for reading and picking out the main points, for synthesis and presentation of information, to practise your skills. The issues and topics must be complex, or dealt with in a complex way at level 3. In each case some possible source documents are given. Remember that you must be able to select your own sources at level 3:

- The religion and customs of a culture different from your own.
  Sources: Encarta, CD-ROMs, books.
- The work of a local wildlife or environment centre within the community.
  Sources: newspapers, brochures, leaflets and fliers.
- Visiting a place of interest in London, and analysing its merits as a tourist attraction.
  Sources: telephone, Internet, newspapers, magazines.
- A recent news issue.
  Sources: newspapers, magazines, library may source these on CD-ROM.
- How local councils work.
  Sources: local council records, leaflets, fliers, brochures, newspapers.
- Planning a trip to Glastonbury festival.
  Sources: telephone, Internet, newspapers, magazines.
- The risk factors associated with coronary heart disease, such as cholesterol, cigarettes, high blood pressure.
  Sources: textbooks, CD-ROM, scientific journals.
- What the fossil record tells us about the history of the earth.
  Sources: text books, Internet sites, Geological museum.

Help desk

Remember in each case you must have a purpose for your reading. This means that you must have a reason for reading. You must say why you need to get the information, and what you will use it for e.g. to write a report, letter or essay; or to make a presentation; to take part in a discussion.

Example:

Local Wildlife or environment centre
Decide:
→ What you will do with the information you find, choose a suitable form and style e.g. report, assignment write up, for use in a presentation.
→ What your sources will be (extended documents are needed, at level 3) e.g. newspaper articles, leaflets from the centre, wildlife trust information, local council documentation.
→ What the key points and ideas are about the way in which the centre works with, and within the community e.g. types of projects, who carried them out, timescales for completion of projects.
→ What arguments and reasons can you find for the success, or otherwise, of the centre and its continued effectiveness within the area e.g. education events, activities for children and families.
→ How to synthesise the information for a purpose e.g. make lists of points and issues, how are they linked, what is the sequence of activities in a successful project, who are the key people who make things happen?
→ The images you will use from your sources e.g. before and after photographs of a clean-up project, local people using a conservation area, taking part in a volunteer day.

Action:
→ Plan the format of your presentation of information.
→ Decide where the images will be used.
→ Produce a draft.
→ Proofread and check your work.
→ Practice if you are making a presentation.
→ Get feedback on your work.
→ Produce a final version.

Communication Part B Tracking and Recording Sheets

Tracking and Recording sheets

Communication Level 3 Part B	Evidence must show you can:
C3.2 Reading and Synthesising Read and synthesise information from two extended documents, about a complex subject including at least one image.	• Select and read material that contains the information you need. • Identify accurately, and compare, the lines of reasoning and main points from text and images. • Synthesise the key information in a form that is relevant to your purpose.

I chose these documents to read: 1
2

I found information from at least
two types of extended
documents:

- Book ☐
- Magazine ☐
- Memo ☐
- Letter ☐

I was trying to find out about:

- Newspaper ☐
- Report ☐
- Article ☐
- Other ☐

The main points I found: 1
2
3

The image I used was a: Picture ☐
Chart ☐
Diagram ☐
Sketch ☐

The point made by the image was:

I synthesised the information for this purpose:

Summary: Some common problems and solutions:

Summary

Problem	Solution
Not being able to decide which documents to read.	Make sure that you have clear instructions about the purpose of your reading. Make a list of possible sources.
Reading things which are not strictly relevant.	Scan and skim documents to pick out the main points, and get the gist of the content.
Choosing areas and points from your reading, which are not strictly needed.	Pick out key words and points as a list. Do not wander from the task/ assignment. Understand what you are reading.
Summary is vague, too long or not clear.	Make short notes. Points must be specific. Put points in order. Understand your notes. Know what your notes are for: use in a discussion, to write a report.
Synthesis does not include your own view.	Identify the main arguments and perspectives of the writers. Analyse their point of view, to decide if you agree. Present your own interpretation of the subject.

If you are having lots of problems, return to step one in Chapter 15. Check your checklists, go to the Help Desks, and ask for advice if you need to, *before* you go on to the next set of practice tasks and assignments.

3.3 Writing

You could use any example of writing, but if you want to use the evidence in your portfolio, someone needs to record your skills as having met the criteria. You can help this process by keeping your own records and reflections of the discussion using the tracking and recording sheets like those which follow on page 224. These sheets can be used to show how your skills are developing. They could also be part of your portfolio evidence, to help show that you can use your skills in different situations.

Remember one of your documents must be extended, and must include an image. The issues and topics must be complex, or dealt with in a complex way at Level 3. You must decide on the format used to present your information effectively. Here are examples of some documents you could write, some of which could be extended:

- Essay on the advantages and disadvantages of genetically modified organisms (GMOs) being used for food (extended document).
- Report on a global conservation project, which has been successfully completed (extended document).
- Letter of application for a full-time job.
- Report on changes in health and safety legislation on work practices in the building trade (extended document).
- Advanced level coursework report or assignment (extended document).
- Letter of application for sponsorship for a university course.
- Assessment of the environmental impact of a new town ring road.
- Flier advertising a disco/party.
- Report on the effects of increasing human populations on world climate (extended document).
- Technical report on the impact of privatisation on passenger and freight rail services (extended document).
- Newsletter covering the sporting, academic, theatrical, and musical achievements of the people in your school/college/organisation.

Example:

Assessment Report of the environmental impact of a new ring road

Proposal for Westwear town ring road
→ The road is to be located around the north of the town, through the villages of Wally and Little Westford.
→ The road is to be built over the next two years, to reduce both the impact of the site works and traffic disruption.
→ The contractor awarded will be required to provide local link roads, set aside and set out an area for local recreation, and set aside a wildlife area with suitable access.
→ The cost of building is to be met by central Government.
→ The parish and district councils are both in favour of the development.

The reasons for having the ring road
→ The new route will vastly improve access to the west of the county.
→ The new route will drastically reduce traffic in the centre of Westwear.
→ Pollution levels in and near the town will be reduced.
→ The centre of town can be pedestrianised for improved access to shops.
→ The road will provide links with part of the national network of motorways, leading to improved communications and transport links for business.

The reasons against having the ring road
→ The new road will generate its own traffic.
→ Rather than easing congestion, traffic levels will increase.
→ The disruption to the village life of Wally and Little Westwood will be considerable.
→ The proposed route has two large badger sites in its path.
→ Pollution levels will increase near the new road, including noise levels.

The costs of the new road, compared with not having one
→ Financially the cost of the new road is £2.2 million, paid for by central Government.
→ Costs in terms of lost business due to poor communication routes are estimated at £0.5 million annually.

Views of local people
→ Local business people are generally in favour, although there are some concerns about the future pedestrianisation project.
→ Local environmental groups are in favour of the new recreation and wildlife sites but against the road itself.
→ Local councils are in favour.
→ Village groups in Wally and Little Westford are strongly against.
→ A questionnaire of inhabitants of Westwear itself showed 53% in favour of the road, £37% against the development, with 10% undecided.

Summary

→ The new road will greatly improve communication routes in the west of the county, and to Westwear.

→ There will be considerable environmental impact around the north of the town, during and after building.

→ The recreation and wildlife areas would be a very positive development in the area.

→ There will probably be an increase in income to the area in business terms.

→ More people are likely to use the new road than current estimates, because it will greatly increase access for those north and west of the town.

→ There is a small majority of local people in favour of the road.

Communication Part B Tracking and Recording Sheets

Tracking and Recording sheets

Communication Level 3 Part B C3.3 Writing

Write two different types of documents about complex subjects. One piece of writing should be extended, and include one image.

Evidence must show you can:

● Select and use a form and style of writing that is appropriate to your purpose and complex subject matter.

● Organise relevant information clearly and coherently, using specialist vocabulary when appropriate.

● Ensure text is legible, and that spelling, grammar and punctuation are accurate, so your meaning is clear.

Document 1	Document 2
Type of document I wrote:	Type of document I wrote:
Letter ☐	Letter ☐
Memo ☐	Memo ☐
Application form ☐	Application form ☐
Notes ☐	Notes ☐
Report ☐	Report ☐

Essay ☐   Essay ☐

The image I have used is: ☐   The image I have used is: ☐

The structure and style of   The structure and style of
document 1 is: ....   document 2 is: ....
....
because...................................   because...................................
....

I have organised my work in the   I have organised my work in the
following way............................   following way............................
....
because...............................   because...................................
....

I have checked my work for   I have checked my work for
spelling, punctuation and grammar: spelling, punctuation and grammar:

Yes ☐   No ☐   Yes ☐   No ☐

I have changed my work to make   I have changed my work to make
sure that it can be easily read by   sure that it can be easily read by
others, and that the meaning is   others, and that the meaning is
clear: clear:

Yes ☐   No ☐   Yes ☐   No ☐

Summary

Some common problems and solutions:

Problems	Solutions
Writing too much, and waffling.	Stick to your list of points. Write in short, clear sentences.
Not using an appropriate style.	Make sure that you understand the task or assignment set, before you begin.
	Be clear in your own mind how you intend to structure your work at the start.
Not structuring work sensibly.	Put your points into order. Use headings and paragraphs to help. Make suitable connections between parts of your work.
	Organise your information in a sensible way.
Not using images sensibly.	Choose a picture, graph or diagram, only if it supports a point which you want to make.
Not proofreading and correcting.	Use a dictionary or spell checker. Check that the relevant rules of grammar and punctuation have been applied.

If you are having lots of problems, return to step one in Chapter 15. Check your checklists, go to the Help Desks and ask for advice if you need to, *before* you go on to the next set of practice tasks and assignments.

16

Communication Level 3: Activities for Assessment of Part B

Portfolio Assignments Level 3

These are further contextualised examples, which can be used as portfolio evidence to meet Part B of the unit requirements. Some of the examples focus on one component of Communication, others are larger, combined assignments.

In Communication you can evidence each component separately, or together.

You should not try to separate the criteria within each component e.g. when you take part in a discussion, you must show that you have:

Made clear, relevant contributions, to suit the purpose and situation

AND

Listened and responded sensitively, and developed points and ideas

AND

Created opportunities for others to contribute.

Help desk

Communication unit: Part B

Has four components or parts at level 3

C3.1a Discussions
C3.1b Presentation
C3.2 Reading
C3.3 Writing

These four parts can be evidenced separately, or together.

Each component, or part, has three criteria. Example: C3.1a Discussions

- Make clear and relevant contributions in a way that suits your purpose and situation.
- Listen and respond appropriately to others and develop points and ideas.
- Create opportunities for others to contribute when appropriate.

These three criteria should not be separated when you produce evidence of your discussion for your portfolio.

There are ideas below for activities, which are designed to evidence separately:

1) Discussions

2) Presentations

3) Reading

4) Writing

There are activities involving:

1) Reading and discussion

2) Reading and presentation

3) Reading and writing

There are activities involving:

1) Discussion, presentation, reading and writing

3.1a Discussions

- Take part in a group discussion on the toxicity and bioaccumulation of pesticides in the environment.
- Take part in a group discussion about the impact of new media technologies on advertising.
- Take part in a group discussion about getting help and information about sexual discrimination.
- Take part in a mock interview for HE entry.
- Take part in a discussion about genocide or ethnic cleansing.
- Discuss inequality in the level of health seen in different groups of people, such as the elderly, children, men, ethnic group, disabled people, women, homeless people, people with low incomes.
- Take part in a discussion in which you analyse the way in which contestants are dealt with in a game show.
- Prepare for a discussion with your supervisor/tutor about the courses you hope to take after your Advanced level courses. Take part in the discussion and evaluate your performance.
- Discuss the role of isolation in the process of speciation.
- You have a part-time job. The hours you work have been arranged around your school/college timetable and study time. Now your employer wants you to work more hours each week, and has said that if you cannot do this, you will be sacked. Take part in a discussion about how to deal with this situation.

Help desk

Places where you take part in discussions, as a part of everyday life, and can practise your skills include: at work, at home, with friends, in a club or society, at church, as part of a political or community group.

3.1b Presentation

- Give a presentation about a residential trip, which has been part of a school or college course.
- Simulate a radio/TV news bulletin.
- Give a presentation about the change in crime rate, and criminal statistics for one type of crime over the last 30 years.
- Present the sequence of events involved in an important scientific or technological discovery of the last 10 years.
- Present a political argument for lowering the current levels of personal taxation in the UK.

3.2 Reading and Synthesising

- Prepare a factual summary of the structure and function of a business use graphs, charts, and diagrams in your report. Present your own views on the financial viability of this business.
- Prepare a summary of local facilities useful to young people, ready to use in a poster, for the 14–19 age group. Try to present the educational facilities in an appealing way, which will encourage young people to get involved.
- Research the history of education, ready to present your findings in an essay, giving your own perceptions of the impact of education on the British economy.
- Compare the safety record for cars and motorbikes. Focus on the data for accidents involving young people under the age of 25 in particular, and any particularly high-risk groups of drivers.

3.3 Writing

- Write an account of a foreign holiday as a diary (extended document).
- Write an information leaflet about the prevention of the spread of HIV, specifically for young people.
- Write an article for a magazine or newsletter about the increase in drug use among young people.
- Write an essay on the history of spoken English.

Help desk

The term C.V. means a summary of:

Your personal details, such as name, address.

Your qualifications.

Details of your education record, such as which schools you attended.

Your other experiences, and responsibilities, such as outdoor pursuits, being a prefect, being a team captain.

Your hobbies and interests, and sporting activities.

Example CV:

Name: Brian Notts
Address: 10 The Close, S. Weatherby, Cornwall EW9 9WE.

Qualifications:

GCSE grades achieved in 1999
English Language B
English Spoken 2
English Literature B
Mathematics B
Science A, A
History B
French C
Geography B
Art and Design B

GCE A level estimated grades for 2000
Biology B
Chemistry C
Geography A

Education:
1995–2000 Weatherby High School, S. Weatherby, Cornwall EW6 6ZZ.

Responsibilities: Library assistant, senior prefect, house captain.

Additional experience:
Work experience placement for three weeks in the county planning office, assisting in drafting county development plans.

Part-time job, for six hours per week, 1999–2001, in McDonalds.

Community volunteer with local conservation group, working on projects to improve a local pond and surrounding area, monitor local bat populations, and remove litter from Sparky Wood.

Hobbies and interests:

I am very interested in environmental and conservation issues. I belong to Greenpeace, and have taken part in several sponsored events to raise funds for international conservation projects, including monitoring turtle populations in the Mediterranean.

I took part in a World Challenge project last Summer, to improve conditions in a school and an orphanage in Peru.

3.1a, 3.2 Reading and discussion

- Prepare for, and take part in, a discussion on the effects of EU membership on the UK economy.
- Prepare for and take part in a discussion on parasitism as a successful way of life, for plants and animals.
- You wish to make a complaint about a product which you have purchased that is faulty. Prepare what you want to say, ready for a telephone discussion with the customer services manager of the company.

3.1b, 3.2 Reading and presentation

- Research the impact of privatisation on passenger and freight rail services. Present your findings to a group of people.
- Research the ways in which cars are advertised, in newspapers, magazines, on radio and TV. Give a presentation on your findings to a group of people.
- Research and present your findings on the increase in cases of TB in the UK in the last 10 years. Are particular socio-economic groups more susceptible than others?
- Research the extent to which our transport policy is sustainable, and sensitive to environmental issues, and present your findings.

3.2, 3.3 Reading and writing

- Research recycling facilities in your area, and make a presentation of your findings as a display for a local library, or in your school or college. Make your display as visually appealing as possible.
- Collect data on one of the following topics, and convert your findings into charts, graphs or diagrams: a survey of the way in which people at your school/college manage their time; unemployment data; sales of mobile phones; increase in traffic on roads.
- You are planning to live away from home, as you start a course at university. Prepare a personal financial plan which will help you budget effectively.
- Design a vehicle to recover equipment left behind at modern battle sites.
- Work out your own fitness schedule to improve your own strength, stamina and flexibility (consult a qualified person before implementing your programme).
- You have been asked to present company figures for the purpose of an end of year meeting of the Board of Directors. Find suitable data on a company, and present the data as bar charts, line graphs, pie charts, in a two-dimensional and three-

dimensional way. Explain why you have presented each set of data in particular ways.

- Research the extent to which our transport policy is sustainable, and sensitive to environmental issues, and present your findings.

3.1a, 3.1b, 3.2, 3.3 Discussion, presentation, reading and writing

Help desk

These are larger projects, tasks and assignments, which may link directly with your curriculum in a school or college. These tasks may also link with the wider aspects of your school or college experience, such as tutorial or careers, or to team sports, drama or musical productions. Some of the tasks link with more general aspects of life experience, or may link to particular areas of business or employment.

- You are organising a conference for a group of teachers, to discuss improving the GCSE A*–C grades achieved at their school. Take part in a discussion about the best way to plan a conference like this. Prepare the following documents for use before and during the conference: fliers for marketing the event; programme; signs for directing people on the day; layout of the rooms and venue. Present your conference planning and preparation to a group of people.
- Plan and design a database using IT, for a club or society to use to keep membership records, and for mailing purposes.
- Plan an event, such as a college disco/birthday party.
- Research and present your findings of the changes in sports and pastimes of a tribal society, as a result of colonialisation.
- Research the use of organic and inorganic fertilisers, as effective and environmentally friendly chemicals, and present your findings.
- Decide on an enterprise project or company, as part of a small group of people. Write a business plan, with financial projections. Present and evaluate your plan.
- Plan and carry out the research and analysis necessary before purchasing a: mobile phone/car/bike/computer/laptop/house. Present your findings.

Example:

Help desk

Planning an event: My Cousin's Wedding

Action Plan for the project:
→ Discuss plan with the bride and groom.
→ Note their requirements.
→ Work out costs.
→ Check within budget.
→ Agree venues, menus, entertainment, guest list, best man, bridesmaids, flowers, photographer, cake, cars, hotels, honeymoon arrangements.
→ Work out timescale for events.
→ Agree timing of the day.

The Bookings to be made:
Agree on providers of services and book:
→ church
→ reception venue
→ evening venue
→ food
→ drink
→ band
→ hire of clothes
→ flowers
→ cake
→ cars
→ photographer
→ hotels
→ honeymoon

Costs of the day:
→ Work out total costs.
→ Review providers and plan if necessary.
→ Work out costs per head.
→ Review guest list if necessary.

Plan for the day:
→ Start time
→ Clothes, hair, cars, flowers
→ Wedding ceremony time
→ Reception time
→ Band time
→ Evening event
→ Departure of bride and groom for honeymoon

17

Communication Level 3: Putting your Portfolio together for Part B

Introduction

This part of the book will help you to plan your assignments, and your portfolio, to meet Part B of the Communication unit. This section also has some record sheets, to help you track your progress. You can use any of the ideas and examples in the first parts of the book to provide evidence. Remember that the contexts in which you developed your skills for Part A should be different to those used to show the application of your skills for Part B. Your portfolio examples are not re-worked or rehearsed, but they show you can build on what you have learned, and apply your skills in new situations.

Planning

This is the process of:
- taking the set task and assignment.
- dividing it up into small steps.
- Keeping it in a timescale.
- Putting it in a sensible order.

The planning process is needed, if you are to structure your work, and do it in a logical order. It will help you keep to deadlines, so you do not have to rush at the end. Look at the box below.

Action Plan:

Task or assignment title:	Dates completed:
What are your action steps?	Target dates for completion:
Who will help you?	
Part B Communication evidence produced: 3.1a	
3.1b	
3.2	
3.3	
IT evidence:	
Application of Number evidence:	
Your signature:	
Assessor signature:	Date:

Review and check progress:

Regularly check back to your plan, to see what you have achieved, and what is left. Are you sticking to time? Are you working in order? What is going well, and what is difficult? Look at the box overleaf for guidance.

Review:

First review:	Date:

With:

Which action steps have you completed?

What has gone well?

What has been difficult?

Any changes made to your plan?

What feedback have you been given?

Which action steps remain/new action steps?	Dates:

What have you achieved?

Part B Communication evidence produced: 3.1a	Dates completed:

3.1b

3.2

3.3

IT evidence:

Application of Number evidence:

Date of next review:

Your signature:

Assessor signature:	Date:

Using your Communication Skills to best advantage:

Performance checklist: Check that you have: Planned your group discussion	Structured your work
Planned your presentation	Written and re-written your work until you are satisfied that it is as good as it can be.
Planned your reading to make best use of the sources of information	Written a memo Written an application form
Made good notes of the main points	Written a letter Written an essay
Written a summary	Written a report
Written a synthesis	

Help desk

Using feedback to improve your work:
You should get regular feedback from your teacher/supervisor. This should be specific, with targets for improvement. Any work not yet finished should be listed with new completion dates.

Portfolio record sheet Level 3

- Use the sheet below to record your portfolio evidence. This should be evidence from tasks, assignments and problem-solving activities to cover part B of the unit. The evidence must reach the standard set out in the Communication unit.
- Your teacher/assessor/supervisor must agree that your evidence reaches the required standard. Remember the contexts recorded here should be different from those used above, to practise and develop your skills for Part A.
- You could use the same activity for several parts of the unit, or you could use different activities for each part.

For Example:

You could find out about the options available to you in education, after Advanced level courses (C3.2), and discuss it with your tutor (C3.1a). You could write a summary of your findings for other people to use (C3.3), and present your findings to others (C3.1b).

You could take part in a group discussion about global warming (C3.1a).

You could make a presentation about a residential trip you have taken part in (C3.1b).

You could find out about local transport services (C3.2).

You could write a report on bias in the media (C3.3).

You will also find that larger contextualised activities will provide opportunities for combined evidence, which can be used as part of your Application of Number and IT portfolios.

Remember do not try to separate the criteria within each component. When you produce some writing, for example, your written evidence must:

Show use of appropriate form and style of writing, for the purpose, on a complex subject

AND

Show clear and coherent organisation of information

AND

Demonstrate that your spelling, punctuation and grammar is accurate.

Tracking and Recording sheets

Communication Part B	Activity I took part in:	Evidence in my portfolio:	Page Number(s)	Date
3.1a Discussions **Group** Complex subject				
3.1b Short talk Lasting more than 5-6 minutes Complex subject Use image(s) to illustrate complex point(s)		Image:		
3.2 Reading and Synthesising Information from two Extended documents, including image(s) Complex subject		Document 1: Document 2:		
3.3 Writing Document 1 on a complex subject				
3.3 Writing Document 2, extended, on a complex subject, with image(s)		Image:		

Portfolio-Building Level 3

The portfolio must show that you have all the skill set out in Part B of the unit. It should show that you can apply your skills in a variety of different situations. Look at the box below for guidance.

- Set up your portfolio at the very beginning.

- Divide the portfolio into: 1) Units
                                2) Components or parts.

- Listen to the guidance given by your teacher/supervisor.

- Remember it is *quality* not *quantity* which is important.

- Choose examples of evidence which prove your skills and knowledge beyond any doubt.

- Do not be afraid to replace early examples of work with better ones from later in your course.

- It is a good idea to include rough or first drafts of a piece of work, labelled as such, with the final version. This shows that this is your own work, and that you planned and developed your ideas.

- Put the unit specifications at Level 3 in the front.

- Include a contents page at the front, which shows the Key Skills units included, and the order of the work.

- Put an index at the start of each Key Skills unit, showing where each piece of evidence can be found.

- Number all the pages. This is the easiest way for anyone to find individual pieces of evidence. I also means that you can use one piece of evidence to meet the requirements of more than one unit.

- Use portfolio records to list your evidence, and to show which part(s) of the standards it meets.

Level 3 Portfolio example layout

Contents page

Name:

Organisation:

Key Skills Units and Levels: Include the Communication Level 3 specifications.

Section 1: Pages 1–32: Communication Level 3.

Section 2: Pages 33–55: Application of Number Level 3.

Section 3: Pages 56–73: IT Level 3.

Index for Communication Level 3.

Page(s)	Communication
1	Portfolio Record Sheet
2–6	3.1: Discussions: Group
7–12	3.1: Presentation
13–17	3.2: Reading
18–25	3.3: Writing: Document 1
26–32	3.3: Writing: Document 2

Examples of evidence for a Level 3 Communication Portfolio

Page 1: Completed Portfolio Record Sheet

Pages 2–6: 3.1 Discussions: Group
>   Pages 2–5: Notes of discussion about the effects of science and technology on the food we eat.
>   Page 6: Observation checklist completed by teacher/supervisor.

Pages 7–12: 3.1 Presentation
>   Pages 7–10: Notes of discussion in my Advanced GNVQ Health & Social Care group about local health care facilities.
>   Page 11: Questions I asked and answered.
>   Page 12: Observation checklist completed by my teacher/supervisor.

Pages 13–17: 3.2 Reading
>   Pages 13–14: The assignment brief with list of books, articles, chapters, and articles I read, with reasons.
>   Pages 15–17: The notes I made about the left and right of politics in Britain today.

Pages 18–25: 3.3 Writing
>   Document 1 The report from my assignment on personal finance and credit facilities available.

Pages 25–32: 3.3 Writing
>   Document 2 The essay on exploitation of the rainforest for general studies.

Glossary

Assessment The ways in which the skills and knowledge you have are tested and marked.

Awarding Body The exam board with whom you are registered, which sets and marks the tests, and checks the portfolio e.g. AQA, ASDAN, Edexcel, OCR.

Candidate Anyone registered for one or more Key Skills units. You must be registered before you can receive a certificate.

Complex You will need to interpret complex subjects and ideas by making sense of several interconnected arguments or concepts and presenting them to others in a clear, uncluttered fashion. You could also deal with a subject, idea or issue in a complex way, perhaps by demonstrating a sensitive approach to the subject. This becomes very important at level 3.

Criteria The standards you must reach in the test, and in your portfolio. If you do not do well enough to meet the criteria you will not get a certificate.

Discussions Taking part in discussions is an important part of the Communication qualification. According to which level you are working at you will be expected to show varying degrees of participation and leadership.

Evidence This could be written work, posters, computer printouts, video, tape, all of which show your skills and knowledge.

External Assessment Test which is either multiple choice at levels 1 and 2, or written at level 2 and 3.

Extended document A document at least three pages long. One of your pieces of writing will need to be an extended document at level 3. It is likely to be a report, an essay, coursework or an assignment.

Feedback Guidance and information provided by your teacher/supervisor. Feedback will help ensure that your work matches the requirements of the Key Skills syllabus.

Internal Assessment The portfolio of evidence.

Images Pictures, charts, diagrams could be inserted as actual images rather than the word description alone.

Level The Key Skill unit Communication can be achieved at levels 1–4.

Portfolio File of evidence which proves the things you say you can do are true.

QCA The Qualifications and Curriculum Authority, the Government organisation which has written the Key Skills units, and has decided on how they should be assessed.

Index